Witty recollections on home-education.

When Rhonda Butterworth suggested removing their children from public school and teaching them at home, her husband, Bill, was a bit skeptical—to put it *mildly*. But Rhonda persisted and Bill later had to admit that their noble experiment in home-education was a smashing success.

In The Peanut Butter Family Home School, Bill Butterworth gives his candid and witty reflections on the rewards of teaching kids at home. With sparkling humor, he reveals that home school is full of surprises, challenges, and blessings. It's a total education experience that's definitely worth the effort.

Whether you send your kids off to school or educate them at home, you'll find lots of chuckles and warm insights on family life in The Peanut Butter Family Home School.

"What's home-schooling really like? Here's a wonderfully human look at the delights and struggles of the Butterworth family. As I read this book on the plane, my emotions ran the gamut from laughing out loud to brushing back a tear."

David R. Mains
The Chapel of the Air

The PEANUT BUTTER FAMILY HomeSchool

BILL BUTTERWORTH

Fleming H. Revell Company
Old Tappan, New Jersey

Unless otherwise identified, Scripture quotations used in this book are from the New American Standard Bible, © The Lockman Foundation 1960, 1963, 1968, 1971, 1972, 1973, 1975, 1977.

Excerpts reprinted from *For the Children's Sake* by Susan Schaeffer Macauley, copyright © 1984. Used by permission of Crossway Books, Westchester, IL 60153.

Material adapted from *The God Hunt*, copyright © 1984 by David and Karen Mains, is used with permission by David C. Cook Publishing Company.

Material from the *Sing, Spell, Read and Write* program, Heads Up, CBN Center, Virginia Beach, VA 23463 is used with permission from the author, Sue Dickson.

Library of Congress Cataloging-in-Publication Data
Butterworth, Bill.
    The peanut butter family home school.

    1. Domestic education—United States—Case studies. I. Title.
LC37.B85   1987   649'.68   87-4886
ISBN 0-8007-5244-9

Copyright © 1987 by Bill Butterworth
Published by the Fleming H. Revell Company
Old Tappan, New Jersey 07675
Printed in the United States of America

It's more than infatuation
More like love and admiration
And a daily realization
That your tireless motivation
Is a cause for celebration
And at least a book dedication
To the consistent inspiration
Behind Union Station Education
So if you need a little translation
And a word about our relation. . .

. . . I love you, Rhonda.
This book is rightfully
dedicated to you.

Contents

Contents

The PEANUT BUTTER FAMILY Home School

 1

Union Station Education

I've always admired the kind of people who give their home a name. That custom has impressed me through the years. Those are the sort of folk who want to create a strong family identity. You know the type of thing I'm talking about—Peaceful Lodge, The Joyful Homestead, Quiet Cottage. Just reading them relaxes you, doesn't it?

Well, the time arrived when we moved our whole family to a bigger house, better suited for our five frantic, frenzied wonderchildren and their magnificent mama. A peaceful, quiet, joyful place on a little street called Union Avenue.

It was a house best described in one word—*potential*. Tucked away in a typical middle-class neighborhood, our new house was a fixer-upper: We could turn four bedrooms into five—with some work. We could take an average-sized kitchen and turn it into a big, beautiful, every-other-woman-would-be-jealous kitchen—with some work. A dining room/family room combination was big enough for our entire family, and it could be given a nice, warm, country feeling—with some work.

It was clearly a "lotsa" move—lotsa kids in the neighborhood, lotsa room in the house, lotsa work to be done, lotsa potential.

Nevertheless, the first thing I did was become the kind of person I admired—I gave our house a name.

What would you call a place that buzzes with activity every day of the year? What name would best suit the home base for five children coming in and out through the screen door seventeen times per minute with gusts of up to twenty-three? Is there a proper title for a place to rest between trips to Little League and ice-skating lessons?

Union Station.

That was it! What else could you possibly call a home that's like a train depot? It fits so well. Our home has all the craziness of a terminal, yet it also provides the place to rest between trips. So it was settled: Union Station.

Life at Union Station is pretty typical. Dad works his job; Mom stays home with the little ones. Ah, yes, the little ones.

Oldest and not so little is our only daughter, Joy. She's a delicate, intricate blend of feelings, a marvelous example of a nine-year-old young woman. She has the energy of a tomboy with the smile of a beauty queen. She loves to skate or swim with her friend Alyson.

Our eldest son is eight-year-old Jesse. He prides himself on having his father's wit (pray for him) and his mother's athletic ability. His white-blond hair tops off a compact package of creativity and confidence. His current love is pitching, catching, and playing first base for his local Little League team.

Jeffrey is six years old, which means his life revolves around GI Joe equipment. He's kind of quiet (a rarity in our house) and loves to imitate people or cartoon them on paper. He can also be known for melting ladies' hearts!

Full speed ahead describes four-year-old John. There's never any doubt where you stand with this little lover. He's straightforward, which drives a lot of folks crazy, but frankly we find it quite admirable. He loves to be read to, and he's, well, quite a special guy.

Rounding out roll call is baby Joseph. "Such a happy baby" or "such a good baby" follow this little guy around. Crawling around with his four-toothed smile, he eats anything in sight.

Oh, there is one aspect of our lives that isn't all that typical—we teach our kids at home. I know what you're thinking . . . *Oh no, one of* **those**! I know *exactly* what you're thinking because, until recently, your thoughts were my thoughts.

Yes, home-education at Union Station has worked out quite nicely. But in order to understand how it works, we'll have to go back to the beginning.

A few years ago *everything* was typical. Wonderfully typical. Joy was in second grade, Jesse was in first, Jeffrey was ready for kindergarten, and John was a toddler. I was pleased to be a parent in an incredibly average home. Families drove station wagons; so did we. Dads wore suits and carried briefcases; so did I. Kids rode bikes and jumped rope; so did ours. Yards had fences; so did ours. And good parents sent their kids to school. So did we.

I had no gripes. Really. I love being average. I don't like to stick out, make waves, or upset the apple cart. Home-schooling didn't fit into my plan. So I never even considered it.

The first germ of the disease came in a letter from a friend of ours. Debbie Woodall was a longtime friend from college days. John, her husband, and she had achieved a goal similar to one of ours: lotsa kids. Her letter was the normal newsy news: This child does this now, this baby is now mobile, this old friend is engaged, and so on.

It was her P.S. that was poison.

P.S.: We're teaching our kids at home and we love it.

When I arrived home from work that night Rhonda met me at the front door. It's always a pleasant sight to see this magical woman who energizes my life. She's a marvelous mixture of so many good things. Small, yet very strong, with pretty blonde hair, electric blue eyes, and that smile that could send me whistling off to Siberia for a bucket of ice. Yes, she really is the human power supply at Union Station. But she's the most beautiful battery I've ever seen.

We kissed and she handed me Debbie's letter. Later, I shared my views with Rhonda.

"So Debbie's a radical now!" I mocked. "What do they do in their home school, collect ammunition and freeze-dried food and store it in their basement for the coming attack?"

"Bill, be nice," Rhonda interrupted.

"Sorry," I whispered.

"I wonder what home-schooling is all about?" Rhonda thought aloud.

"Whoa, whoa, sweetie pete," I protested. "Don't get any ideas. There's no way we're gonna get into that stuff.

Besides, it's probably illegal, and I'm not going to jail over such a silly issue."

Rhonda sat quietly.

"So that's the end of that," I stated emphatically.

I should have known better.

The next few weeks saw the continued curiosity of a woman born to mother. Rhonda began poring over books on the home-school movement with a real fervor. As her excitement grew, I was having my own emotional increase: I was in a panic.

"Isn't life beautiful!" I began one afternoon. "The weather is beautiful, the sun is shining, the children are healthy, those who are supposed to be in school *are*," I further emphasized. I ended by heaving a dramatic sigh of contentment, just for the added effect.

"Yes, if life was meant to be without challenge, we sure have the best of it." Rhonda's words pierced the peace.

I sat in awkward silence for a couple of minutes that felt like a dozen decades.

"I like things the way they are," I weakly protested. "Why rock the boat?"

"There are tons of good reasons for teaching your kids at home," Rhonda stated in a calm, matter-of-fact tone. "But I think this is really bringing out a big difference in our basic approaches to life."

I reacted as I usually do whenever Rhonda makes a heavy, philosophical statement of this nature: My eyelids began blinking.

"Now don't just sit there blinking at me," she protested. "You like things the way they are because you are satisfied with more predictable living. I think home-schooling would be a wonderful dimension to add to our family life for lots of reasons, not the least of which is the challenge it would bring to our lives."

I slumped down in my chair. I knew I was in for the old "Pioneer Spirit" talk. All I could think of was the theme song from "The Waltons," and the life-sized poster of Michael Landon down at the camera store.

"Where's your pioneer spirit?" Rhonda recited. "Where would this country be if our forefathers had settled for average living?"

I thought, *We'd be thirteen colonies still under the rule of England.*

"Why, we'd be thirteen colonies still under the rule of England!" Rhonda answered her own question. "What if America were filled with mediocre people? There would have been no Tom Edisons, Abe Lincolns, Wright Brothers, Ben Franklins, or Eleanor Roosevelts!"

I prayed to God that she would stop there, resisting the temptation to get into thirty-one flavors and cable TV. But it's the prayer of a *righteous* man that avails much.

"Would there be thirty-one flavors of ice cream if life were average? No. What would we have?"

"Vanilla," I answered on cue.

"Right. Would we have the Disney Channel, ESPN, or any other cable television offers if we were satisfied with the normal?"

"No, we would only have ABC, NBC, and CBS," I piped in. "See, I read *Megatrends* too!"

I fell right into her trap.

"Great, then you're aware of the exciting entrepreneurial spirit sweeping our country today. Think of the movement toward cottage industries!"

"You mean business at home?" I asked.

"Exactly. Home-schooling is the ultimate cottage industry. Our business as parents is to educate our children." Rhonda stopped and smiled, apparently pleased with what she said.

"Do you feel qualified to teach?" I asked, trying another tactic.

"Yes and no," was her diplomatic response. "I don't have a teaching degree, and that makes me feel less qualified. But you *have* a degree in education; do you feel qualified because of it?"

My honest answer was no, but I just motioned for her to go on, since I didn't want to cloud the issue with my own inadequacies.

"But on the other hand," she continued, "who is better qualified to teach children than their parents? Nobody knows them better. It's a great way to exercise the special wisdom God gives you for your own family."

Boy, I thought, *she really is on a roll. I gotta think fast.* Suddenly it came to me.

"SOCIALIZATION," I blurted out.

Rhonda jumped. It wasn't the word that startled her as much as me screaming it out.

"What?"

"Socialization," I repeated. "If we keep the kids home from school, they won't get a chance to socialize. It may help them academically, but they will shrivel up socially."

As I beamed with pride, Rhonda yelled to Jeffrey through the screen door. "Jeffrey, are you and John having fun playing together?"

"YEAH."

"Where's Joy?"

"She's over with Danielle and Angie."

"Where's Jesse?"

"Playing with Chris and Derrick—"

"Okay."

". . . and Bruce and Bill and Damon—"

"Thank you."

". . . and Stacy and—"

17

"Okay, okay!" I interrupted.

Rhonda continued, "With four kids of our own, thinking about more, and all the neighbor kids, and church, and play group, and Care Bear Club, and children's choir, are you really worried about our children socializing?"

I blushed. I hate it that I turn red when I'm whipped. Boy, I was whipped. Boy, I was red.

"So all people who send their kids to school are Mr. and Mrs. Mediocre, right?"

"Wrong," said Rhonda. "There you go generalizing again. Home-schooling isn't the way for everybody, but I really feel it is right for us. I think it can bring our family together in ways we've never imagined. A child's early years are so important. I want to be in on their total development—physically, emotionally, socially, mentally, and spiritually. It goes far beyond academics. I can't speak for others. Good parents send their kids to school and it's just fine, but I'm feeling more and more discomfort handing Joy and Jesse over to a school for six hours a day."

She was serious. Her look told me this was more than a fad, a fling, or a fancy. This was an issue of importance.

"Maybe we should get some wise counsel from an educator," I suggested. "I'd feel better if we heard about this issue from someone qualified in the field."

"All right," agreed Rhonda. "But who?"

I thought for a moment, scratching my head. "How about Mr. Stewart, the principal at Joy and Jesse's school?"

Rhonda's eyes lit up. "David Stewart! He'd be perfect! He'd give us the straight scoop. Call him up and see what he has to say."

The next morning I called and arranged to meet David Stewart for lunch on Tuesday of the following week. I felt real good about talking with David. I still had serious doubts about this entire issue, and I just knew that David could give me the ammunition I needed for my attacks on Rhonda's position.

So as the week went by, I allowed Rhonda to feel she had the winning argument. As any good husband knows, you get along much better this way.

Tuesday arrived and I picked up David promptly at 11:30 A.M. at his office on the school's campus. We chit-chatted in the car all the way to the restaurant. The hostess seated us, the waitress took our order, I thanked God silently for this magic moment of victory, and I started in on David.

I cleared my throat and began. "David, I've got something really crazy to discuss with you. Rhonda and I have been talking about something lately that needs the kind of objective counsel you could bring."

I really had his curiosity aroused at that point. Inside I was jumping up and down, knowing that across the table sat all the objections to home-schooling in one man's body. *Thank You, Lord, for this opportunity*, I silently prayed. *David is truly sent to us from You. I am willing to put all my eggs in one basket and go with his feelings about home-schooling. Please help Rhonda to feel the same way. Amen.*

The silent prayer supercharged me even more. I was now ready to drop the bomb on David.

"David," I said, leaning over the table for heightened effect, "what if I told you that Rhonda and I are thinking of pulling Joy and Jesse out of your school and, instead, teaching them at home?"

There was a glazed look on David's face.

He's not the kind of guy to just spout off an answer under normal conditions, so I knew he'd take some time over this missile. I was right.

Finally, when a pause that seemed endless ended, he said, "Well, I'd be shocked."

I smiled. I wanted to rub my hands together in fiendish glee, but I restrained myself. "I figured you'd respond like this, David," I comforted.

"But you don't understand why I'm shocked," he interrupted.

Thoughts ran through my mind of feeding facts to Rhonda that would silence her scream forever. I was just about to ask David for the good stuff when he opened his mouth and volunteered the reason behind his shock.

"I'm shocked over this whole issue because—" David paused—"because I think it's the most WONDERFUL OPPORTUNITY YOU AS PARENTS WILL EVER EXPERIENCE!"

He beamed. I bawled. He went on. I wiped up.

"I guess I get especially excited over the prospect of home-schooling for a very personal reason," continued my ex-friend David.

"What's that?" I peeped.

"Well, it just so happens that I was taught at home until I was in the eighth grade."

He smiled. I scowled. He continued sincerely. I cried silently.

"I feel that my education at home was the best thing that happened to me in my entire childhood!"

"Does this mean you would recommend it?" I dumbly asked, fearful of the obvious.

"By all means! I'd not only recommend it, I'll do whatever I can to assist you in pulling it off. I'm sure Rhonda would enjoy some of the resources the school could offer her in her teaching."

"I'm sure she'll be very excited to hear about all this," I said with the enthusiasm of a mortician.

"Well, I know I'm very excited!" David exclaimed. "This reminds me of the pioneer spirit that made America great!"

Oh no, I thought. *Here comes Pioneer Spirit: Part Two.* I decided to jump right in to speed it up. I silently climbed up Walton's Mountain.

"Yeah, that great American spirit of challenge," I said with a careful blend of cynicism and sincerity. "Guys like Thomas Edison—"

"Did you know he was taught at home?" David interjected.

"Uh, uh, no, uh, I didn't," I mumbled. I couldn't believe this was happening to me. I moved quickly through the list. "And Abe Lincoln—"

"Home-taught as well," remarked David.

"The Wright Brothers."

"Yes, that's right, two more examples of time spent in home-schooling."

"Ben Franklin?"

"You're batting a thousand!" David cheered. "All those men had a portion of their education in the home-school setting."

I whispered out the last name from Rhonda's Pioneer Spirit lecture. "Eleanor Roosevelt?"

"No, I'm afraid she wasn't home-schooled, to my knowledge."

I sighed. A ray of sunshine in the home-school storm.

"However," David went on to say, "her husband, Franklin, was another product of home-schooling, so that should help you in your thinking!"

"Yes, this really has been a big help," I stated from my state of shock. "You have no idea what this has done for me, my wife, and our kids."

"Well, you certainly won't be alone," David encouraged. "I was reading the *Wall Street Journal* recently and they cited some authorities who estimate there are somewhere between a half million to one million children being home-schooled in the United States!"

He laughed. I lamented. He ate. I abstained. He partied. I paid.

After I drove him back to his school, I went to the office, put in my afternoon of work, and realized that when I returned home that evening it would no longer be to a suburban home in Southern California. No, lunch had settled my fate. God had answered my prayer. That evening I pulled my car into the driveway of . . .

. . . the Little House on the Prairie to begin observing the inevitable changes taking place in the lives of my kids and their mama—a home-school pioneer parent.

2

Heppie
Bread

I still had serious doubts.

Pioneer spirit was a good idea, but there had to be more to this whole home-schooling idea to give it the staying power it needed to make it at Union Station. As I took the next few days to review what all this new information was going to mean, I recalled an aspect of Rhonda's Pioneer Spirit talk that had fascinated me.

She had called home-schooling the "ultimate cottage industry." That concept was growing on me, appealing to the entrepreneur inside of me. I just wasn't sure how this little home business was going to manifest itself.

Our evening meal is always an appropriate time for a discussion. Our white pine dining room table, complete with extra leaves for maximum space, sat in the center of our dining room. Rhonda sat at one end of the table and I sat at the other. Joy and Jesse were to my right and Jeffrey and John were to my left.

The smell of baked chicken and rice was filling the house with splendor. There is always such a warm, friendly feeling in this place. And Rhonda is always personally responsible for that fact.

During that time, teaching our kids at home became the main topic in just about every conversation our family conducted. So one night at dinner I decided to get into "Entrepreneuring Education."

"Babe, pass the broccoli puff, please, and tell us more about Union Station Education being a cottage industry."

Rhonda passed the puff to Jesse, who took the liberty of shoveling generous portions on his plate. "Well," she began slowly, "it's like I said the other day. Our business as parents will be to educate our children, and in that sense it is the ultimate cottage industry."

"Mama, are we becoming a business?" Jesse interrupted as he passed a noticeably lighter broccoli puff casserole dish to Joy.

"No, not really," responded Rhonda. "Our business is simply to teach you and your brothers and sister all we can about life, so in the truest sense we're not a business."

"But if we're gonna learn 'bout life, I think we should learn 'bout business too!" It was Jeffrey, piping in with one of his little gems. Everyone giggled at the thought of a little preschooler wanting to discover debits and ponder profits.

It was Rhonda who stopped laughing before everybody else. "You know, Jeffrey, you might not be too far off from a good idea!"

Jeffrey beamed with pride as he was handed an almost-empty casserole dish.

"Tell us!" I begged. "Don't keep us in suspense! What is Jeffrey's not-too-far-from-good idea?"

"I was reading a book on home-schooling yesterday," she began. "And it was very emphatic on using the everyday experiences around the house as teaching times."

"Like what?" I asked.

"Oh, stuff like letting the young child set the table and, in doing so, the child must count out the correct number of plates, glasses, big people's silverware, children's utensils, and so on."

"I see," I chimed in. "The kid gets an effective real-life situation in arithmetic."

"They don't call it 'mithatick anymore, Dad," Joy interjected. "Today they call it *math*."

Now I was not only confused, I was also prehistoric.

"I'm still missing something here, babe," I continued. "What's this leading up to?"

"I guess I'm just thinking out loud, but another area of this use of everyday experiences is in the kitchen . . . you know, preparing food for the meals. More good math training as they measure ingredients to make certain things. Even fractions, as they deal with half a cup of this and a quarter of a cup of that."

"Go on," I prompted. She really had my attention aroused. Her verbal thinking always amazes me.

"Well, you know how I like to bake homemade bread." She was abruptly interrupted by cheers and applause for a product that was well loved and quickly consumed at Union Station.

"Anyway, the kids and I would bake loaves of bread and sell them to friends and neighbors. Both the baking and the business would teach them a lot about life."

I was suddenly overcome with exhilaration and depression. I was exhilarated over the potential represented in Rhonda's entrepreneurial plan. I was depressed because

Jeffrey handed me a casserole dish that was not only empty, but *licked* clean.

"Well, it's clear to me you're a good cook," I began, still lamenting my loss of broccoli puff. "Your bread is a winner. I know it would sell. What do you kids think about this idea?"

"It tastes good to me!" came from Jesse.

"I'm gonna be a businessman!" stated Jeffrey, still aware he was in on the groundbreaking of this enterprise.

"Yummy Bread," was all we could get from John, totally immersed in his meal. As I looked at him, I spied a morsel of broccoli puff on the table, beside his plate. *I'll get that later,* I thought.

"Does this mean we'll get money for our bread?" asked Joy. When I nodded, she lit up and said, "Oh boy, I think I'm going to really like home-schooling. Jesse, we're gonna be rich!"

I was about to correct her when I realized she felt rich with two quarters in her little purse. I decided to let her stay excited.

"Bill, this has real possibilities," Rhonda stated. "This is what total education is all about. We can teach the kids math, business, baking, and have a lot of fun in the process."

"Tom Edison was home-schooled!" I suddenly blurted out. "I wonder if he tinkered around with electric stuff before he made it big?" I was really getting excited. "Baked bread today, the *Fortune* 500 tomorrow. Watch out, *Wall Street Journal*. Save us some space on your front page—six young entrepreneurs who call themselves the Union Station Education Company have arrived!"

"It's discovering the adventure of life!" echoed a motivated mama.

"They can stop searching for excellence; it's right here!" I replied.

"We'll start our own movement!"

"That's right," I replied. "*Y*oung *I*nexperienced *B*akers—we can call ourselves YIBBIES!"

"Hurray for the YIBBIES!" cheered the kids.

"Wait a minute!" I exclaimed. "Yibbies are really just a select group of people from the whole home-school population. What we really need now is a name for that group."

"How 'bout Home-School People?" was Jesse's suggestion.

"That's close, Jess," I encouraged. "How about Home-Educated Person? We would call ourselves HEPPIES!"

And with that conversation we witnessed the birth of Heppie Bread.

In the days ahead, Heppie Bread became hard work for Rhonda and heaven for her hubby. I don't believe there is any reference in the Bible to what heaven will *smell* like, but I'm convinced it will smell like fresh-baked bread. There's just nothing to compare with that arresting aroma. "Kinda makes a guy wanna stick around more," I teased Rhonda one lunch hour when I came home for some quick time with my merry band of bakers.

Rhonda gave me her "Oh, brother!" look, but I knew she was glad to hear my silliness anyway.

But there was more to my heavenly experience than that which entered my sniffer. There was a sight to be seen that is also best described as "heaven." I'm referring to the delight of watching a family work together.

The kitchen was a blur of activity. Joy was measuring ingredients; Jesse was preparing the baking pans; Jeffrey was holding onto the yeast packets as though they would fly away if he let them go. John was in charge of passing things. And this little description wouldn't be complete without one more important element: There was whole wheat flour everywhere! It was sort of a snowstorm with tan snow. Beige haze.

Our little butcher-block kitchen was becoming an institution of higher learning. The students were learning
about temperature. They were learning about yeast. They
were learning fractions, multiples, and most of all team-
work!

They all worked feverishly to prepare the mixture.
Then they hit the real fun: kneading the dough. Now
honestly, can you think of anything more enjoyable for
four kids than the opportunity to get their little hands on
a concoction as strange as bread dough?

"Gee, it feels really weird," pronounced Joy, with a
very distorted expression on her face.

"Gooey," was Jeffrey's one-word description.

"Are you sure this stuff will turn out to be bread?"
asked Jesse.

"I like it just like this," came the word from John
through a Cheshire grin. "It's funner to eat."

After a quick description of what unbaked bread can do
to a little tummy, we started to see more dough in the
baking pan where it rightfully belonged. "It's still funner
to eat," mumbled John in a successful attempt to have
the last word.

As the four of them passed the baking pans to Mom one
by one in bucket-brigade style, I reflected on how special
this enterprise was to our family. The issue wasn't getting rich by selling bread; it was the rich experience in
making the bread. Looking at this picture-perfect scene
in our kitchen, I thought, *If this were a movie, there would
be a soft, fuzzy border around the screen.*

When I came back into focus in our kitchen, I realized
I *was* seeing a soft, fuzzy look to this episode. Taking my
glasses off to rub my eyes, I discovered the cause of this
theatric effect—whole wheat flour on my glasses.

The bread baked, the Heppies entertained heaven in
their respective noses and waited for the timer to

announce the arrival of hard work in a loaf. Jeffrey set the timer, which was quite an arithmetic—er, excuse me, *math*—lesson for a little guy just learning his numbers.

The arrival was near. The kids simulated a countdown. I think John fully expected the bread to blast off out of the oven.

"Ten, nine, eight, seven," they all shouted in joyful anticipation.

"Six, five, four."

Rhonda and I winked at each other, with ear-to-ear smiles.

"Three, two, one, BLAST OFF!!!"

"ONNNNNKKKK."

Our timer buzzer was right on. Mama was in charge of removing the evidence from its incubator. She methodically took each baking pan over to a spot on the kitchen counter predetermined to be the "Cooling Corner."

The kids were dancing around like chimney sweeps in *Mary Poppins*. Rhonda was proudly examining the fruit of her labors, and I was simply taking deep breaths of air, drinking it all in.

After the bread cooled, it was removed from its pan and given a new home in a tinfoil wrap. I glanced at my watch and realized it was time for me to go back to the office. My taunt about sticking around more was nothing but the truth. I was rediscovering my family in a whole new light.

"Well, I hate to say this, but I have to go back to work. My lunch hour is over," I announced in a tone that genuinely demonstrated my disappointment.

"That's okay, babe," reassured Rhonda. "We were just about to leave, too."

"Oh?" I quizzed. "Where are you headed?"

"We're off to create some consumers, right, kids?"

"You better believe it!" came the voices of four satisfied customers.

Rhonda continued, "There's the Campbells, the Hogelands, the Sanders, Hank and Marilyn, the Ludlums, Rae, Ad and Jocelyn, the Keys, Terry and Debra, John and—"

"Whoa!" I interrupted. "Are you going to visit all those people?"

"Eventually," was the reply of one special lady.

"I love it when you're determined," I whispered as I hugged her tightly.

"Are you proud of us?" she asked.

"Are you kidding?" I reassured. "I don't care if we don't make one penny on this experiment, you'll always be my all-time favorite entrepreneur."

We kissed and headed our separate ways. As my crew drove off, I could just envision Jesse walking up to our friends and saying, "Hey, you better buy this bread 'cause we made it ourselves and it's the best bread in America and we're learning how to do this stuff at home and we want your money!" I smiled as I thought of Rhonda clarifying the issue for our friends so they'd remain our friends.

I could end the chapter here and leave you with the illusion that this small business took off and I quit my job in order to handle the two thousand orders we receive daily. But that wouldn't be fair, because it wouldn't be true.

No, Heppie Bread is still small-time. Let's face it, had you ever heard of it before you read this chapter?

But who's to say what's ahead? Union Station Education is total education that doesn't reveal itself in one project. It's a long-term commitment to the business of teaching our kids. So, I realize it'll take quite a bit of time to fully discover all the possibilities represented in this enterprise. Edison dabbled with hundreds of experiments before he saw the light. Maybe Heppie Bread is still ahead of its time. There are always chocolate chip cookies, homemade pizza, bran muffins, or any of the hundred other recipes possessed by my sweetie. The key is, *we gave it a try* and the kids were a vital part of the process.

Back in the car, heading for the office, I tapped the steering wheel while waiting for the longest red light in our little town. As I looked up at the dashboard my eye caught the Xerox copy of an excerpt from a book Rhonda was reading on home-schooling—*Better Late Than Early*. The author is Raymond Moore, who I soon discovered was a recognized authority in the field of home education.

Rhonda had the following section highlighted with a yellow marker:

> One of the best ways for parents to help in their children's social development is to become involved with them in the daily chores and activities of the home. Such lessons of love and responsibility take time and patience, but in performing duties about the home, children learn how to work and how to relate to work. Even in babyhood, the child can help mother make the bed by fluffing the pillows or straightening the blankets. The parent's patience in sharing these duties will be richly rewarded as the child develops a positive sense of self-worth.

I was rudely interrupted by the honking of horns behind me. The light was green.

At the next red light I pressed on in the excerpt:

> Many children are setting the table and removing the dishes by age 3 or 4, and washing them and putting them away by age 5 or 6. And some chil-

dren—boys and girls—are trained to prepare an entire meal or wash the car thoroughly by 7 or 8. Some of the best bread we have ever tasted was baked by an eight-year-old.

"Ha!" I laughed out loud. "You've never tasted Heppie Bread, Dr. Moore!"
The last paragraph coincided with the last red light:

The time parents invest in this kind of education brings the nearest thing to happy, and trouble-free futures, *especially if the parents work with the children.* In addition, the child is learning information traditionally associated only with the school experience. He may read from cereal boxes or count cups and spoons when setting the table. He delights in measuring ingredients for recipes. He enjoys weekly trips to the supermarket, where he begins to learn how to price foods.

This home-school stuff is really kind of captivating, I thought as I neared the office. *It brings together the challenge of Pioneer Spirit and the energy of entrepreneuring.*
I pulled up to the office parking lot and chuckled aloud. My pioneer spirit vision of Michael Landon had been bumped by an image of Big Business 1980s style.
In my mind's eye all I could see was Lee Iacocca standing next to a loaf of Heppie Bread saying, "If you can find a better loaf of bread . . . buy it."

Home-School Trivial Pursuit

The announcement of the birth of Union Station Education was met with mixed reaction. Many of our friends, neighbors, and relations are as crazy as we are, so they applauded us on our willingness to explore uncharted turf.

But there were other friends, neighbors, and relatives who were less enthusiastic:

"How can you WILLINGLY deprive your kids of the education this great country affords them?"

"You isolationists! Don't you want your children to see what life is all about? In the REAL WORLD?"

"It's illegal! See you in jail, sucker!"

It was this sort of encouragement that added daily to my unsettled feeling. I was like a Ping-Pong ball, being hit from one side to the other on the table of home-school debate.

Since I had spent so many years in educational settings, teaching full-time for eight years and part-time for four, many of my friends had questions about the academic issues. As hard as I tried to talk to them about "total education," they kept coming back to the "nuts and bolts" as they would call it . . . reading, writing, arithmetic, and the like. They'd pelt me with questions: "What subjects do you teach?" "Does Rhonda do long-range lesson planning?" "How about daily lesson plans?" "Are all your kids at grade level?" "Do they overlap subjects or are they all taught separately?" "Can you describe to me some of her teaching techniques?"

These were the types of questions I'd be asked, and I'd always respond with the same depth of knowledge: "I dunno."

So, I hurriedly scribbled down all these questions on the back of a Publishers Clearing House envelope. The contest was built for folks with shorter names, since it said, "You may already have won a million dollars, Mr. Butterwort!" Woe to all of us with more than ten letters in our last names. Anyway, I managed to squeeze all the questions on the back of the envelope, except for the last question about teaching techniques, which I wrote around Ed McMahon's head.

When I came home from work that evening, Rhonda asked sweetly, "How was your day, sweetie?"

I smiled weakly at her. "It was fine at work, but I've been mulling around several questions about the academic nuts and bolts of home-schooling."

Rhonda reached out, gave me a big hug, and gently whispered in my ear, "You've been talking to your friends again, haven't you?"

I blushed and nodded.

"Well, I'm gonna make a believer out of you yet!" she declared with a real sense of mission. I continued to blush. Her short blonde hair and blazing blue eyes always reminded me of a perky college cheerleader, and her last statement had all the makings of a winning cheer.

She continued, "So after dinner, let's sit down at the dining room table and talk through your questions, okay?"

I nodded in agreement.

"I suppose that's why you're carrying around that Publishers Clearing House envelope that's sticking out of your jacket pocket. The questions are on the back of it, right?"

I nervously fumbled with my sport coat in order to shift the envelope back into its desired position. I hate it when she's always right, so I replied:

"No, it just so happens that Ed McMahon was at the office today, passing these out!"

She snickered and snapped back mischievously, "So did you win a million today, Mr. Butter*wort?*"

I gobbled my dinner, in order to get to the Home-School Trivial Pursuit contest I was about to employ. I eat fast normally, but this meal was inhaled.

Dinner done, dishes cleared, dining room hosed down, I sat down and carefully unfolded my envelope containing the evening's agenda.

"Okay, question number one," I began. "Where do you have school?"

"Right here," she replied, patting her hand on the dining room table.

I looked around. *I love this room,* I thought. Our dining room is a portion of a big room we use for both dining room *and* family room. It is decorated in "Country Rhonda." The entire room is paneled in warm knotty pine. The vaulted ceiling gives it an even larger feel than its dimensions. The floor is tiled in brick red squares with blue braided area rugs under the pine dining room table and over in the family room area.

The north wall looked like a typical classroom wall in any school. On the wall hung a blackboard, a poster containing the alphabet in printing, and a poster with the alphabet in cursive.

Rhonda had a small desk up against the wall, complete with piles of books, notebooks, pencils, markers, construction paper, flash cards, and, of course, a globe.

My mental tour of the school was interrupted by the tour guide's familiar voice. "In the winter, I'd like to do some of our reading over in the living room, in front of a crackling fire in the fireplace."

We both smiled, as the thought of our children reading by the fire conjured up feelings of peace and serenity. I had to force myself back to the Clearing House questionnaire.

"All right," I mumbled, as I scribbled down the answer, "you do the teaching here at the dining room table, which the kids use as their desk, correct?"

"Correct. And here in the dining room, they can use the chalkboard for math problems or handwriting exercises or drawing."

"Chalkboard for math problems . . . ," I mumbled as I filled the envelope and moved on to a notepad for the continuing answers. I finished writing and returned to the envelope.

"Question two. What subjects do you teach?"

"Math, science, reading, writing, spelling, music, art, California history, and the presidents of the United States. This corresponds to the minimum courses of study that many states require. Each state is different—as you know—but this is the general consensus on subject matter."

I was writing furiously. "All right," I said slowly, as I finished up, "how much time do you devote to each subject?"

Rhonda paused and put her finger to her cheek as she thought this one through. "That's a tough one because it tends to vary with the particular subject and the particular child. That's the advantage of this tutorlike relationship. But if I had to generalize, I guess we average about twenty minutes on a given subject."

"Do you overlap subjects or teach each child separately?" I asked, never looking up from my notes.

"Both," she replied. "Joy, Jesse, and Jeffrey all get the same in music, California history, and the presidents. And they all have separate levels in reading, spelling, and math."

"That brings us to question five," I said as I checked my notes. "Do you use long-range lesson planning?"

"Yes, I do," she came back quickly. "And I use daily lesson plans as well. All the authorities in education agree: Whether at home or in a classroom, proper lesson planning helps incorporate sequential review, sets standards for each lesson, clarifies objectives, motivates the teacher and the student, provides data for performance feedback, and aids in providing the necessary close for the lesson."

"Oh, that's good," I cheered. "That's the next question—daily lesson plans."

Rhonda got up from the dining room table and went over to her desk. She produced three lesson-plan books, each with a different child's name on it.

"I do long-range lesson planning by the month," she commented as she passed me Joy's book. "Here's what's listed for Joy in September."

The book was opened to a page entitled *September*. It was divided up into boxes—one box for each subject.

"I think I'll just jot some of this down in case I want to

refer to it," I said, once again beginning to write frantically.

"You mean you'll copy it down to show your skeptical friends," Rhonda taunted with the truth.

She had a box for language. In the box she had written, *Sentences, Capitalization, End Marks.*

"What does this mean?" I asked, pointing to the language box.

Rhonda pulled the plan book over so she could see it. "It means we'll be reviewing the components of sentence structure, capitalization of names and beginnings of sentences, and end marks—periods, question marks, and exclamation points."

I was grunting and "uh-huh"ing as I was getting this all down on paper. I turned my attention to the box for math. It had words like *Review Addition, Subtraction, Multiplication for 0, 1, 2, Measurements, Time, Money,* and *Place Value.*

"Joy will move into parts of speech in October. Nouns, verbs, and all that good stuff." Rhonda was unaware that I had moved to the math box.

"I'm looking at math," I replied as I was racking my brain trying to remember what *place value* meant. Out of desperation I finally admitted my ignorance.

"I give up. Refresh my memory. What does *place value* mean?" I asked, shrugging my shoulders.

"You remember," Rhonda began by teasing. "Ones, tens, hundreds, thousands—the columns for the number."

"Oh, of course," I laughed. "How silly of me to forget that key concept."

"I was doing some reading about place value," Rhonda continued. "The trick for kids Joy and Jesse's age is to get them to understand how to write numbers like 2,804. If they don't understand it, they'll put the four in the tens column."

I smiled and skipped down the remaining boxes. They all followed the same basic order. Since we did one president a week, the September presidents' box read, *George Washington, John Adams, Thomas Jefferson, James Madison.*

The same pattern was developed for California history—one chapter a week from the textbook. The words in the box were *California Indians, Spanish California, California under Mexico,* and *California Gold Rush Days.*

My eyes skimmed down to the box for music. I grinned as I finally saw something familiar. I helped Rhonda pick out four composers for a music appreciation type of course. I picked four musicians from four periods of history. But I also thought each of these four men would especially excite one of our kids.

I flashed back to the fun of picking out the music at the record store.

I chose Bach for Joy Lynn. He can be soft and gracious in his style. She would especially enjoy "Jesu, Joy of Man's Desiring." The tape I bought had his Toccata and Fugue in D Minor on side two for extra good measure.

I felt Jesse would particularly enjoy Beethoven. I picked something that emphasized his boldness in his music: Symphony No. 5 in C Minor, op. 67.

Jeffrey, being our complex little man of mystery, was a natural for Tchaikovsky. I found a great tape with the 1812 Overture, op. 49; March Slav, op. 31; Fantasy Overture, *Romeo and Juliet;* and *Sleeping Beauty,* op. 66 Waltz on it.

Something with clear energy was needed to capture Johnny's attention. Who could do a better job than another John—Sousa! "The Stars and Stripes Forever," "El Capitan," "Washington Post," "High School Cadets," and "Semper Fidelis" would keep my little guy in gear.

September's box simply stated *Bach.* So I made myself

return to the present. We'd listen to one composer a month on a regular basis. I knew in time we'd grow to appreciate all of them.

We had the same plan for art appreciation as well.

"There's a great idea that's going to provide a lot of help in linking the artists, composers, presidents, and California history all together." Rhonda beamed with pride as she spoke. "It's not listed there on the plan book, but it's exciting to me!"

"What is it?" I asked, my curiosity sufficiently aroused.

"Clothesline," was the reply.

"Clothesline?"

"Yes. We're going to make a time line out of clothesline over here on this wall," she explained, while pointing to the chosen wall in the dining room. "We have a set of flash cards for all the presidents that we'll hang up with clothespins, one per week. We'll get the pictures of the artists, composers, and bits of California history and place them at the appropriate spots along the clothesline. The educational value of bringing all these subjects together is fabulous!"

My pen almost had a blowout, I was writing so fast.

"I have long-range lesson plans for Jesse and Jeffrey as well," Rhonda said while passing me two other books.

"That's okay," I replied. "I believe you. Let's look at some daily lesson plans for Joy, while I'm in tune with her studies."

Rhonda agreed without argument. She put the boys' lesson books aside and turned to the daily-lesson-plan section of Joy's book.

Now, here were the nuts and bolts of the academics. The lesson-plan book had its now familiar boxes again on this page. But instead of months, here it was one day per box.

One day's entry for language read *Sentence Definition,*

Fragment Definition. The math box read *How many hours in a day? How many minutes in an hour?* All the boxes had references back to the textbook for the particular subject, such as *Fragments—page 5.*

"This stuff is really something," I confessed. "I'm impressed."

Rhonda smiled. "As all teachers say, 'It always looks good in the lesson book!' "

"Well, tell me, how do you actually teach this stuff?" I asked in sincere tones. "Take sentences and fragments as an example. How do you teach that?"

Rhonda returned to her desk and located Joy's language book.

"Joy uses this workbook." Rhonda presented me with her book. "Here's what I did in the definition of a sentence. The first thing is for *me* to read it to her."

I nodded as she cleared her throat. With great expression she read: "A sentence is a group of words that expresses a complete thought. It begins with a capital letter and usually ends with a period."

I applauded her for her energy level. "A grand performance!"

"After I read it to her, then *she* reads it to me," she continued. "Then, she writes it in her notebook. Finally, she goes to the pages in her workbook that give her exercises to do to be certain she's mastered the concept."

She paused for breath, but quickly added, "This goes on throughout the year: sentences, fragments, declarative sentences, interrogative sentences, imperative sentences, exclamatory sentences—"

"I get the picture, babe," I interrupted. "You really have this organized, that's for sure!"

"Well, do you have enough ammunition to respond to your skeptical friends, or shall I tell you about Jesse's cursive handwriting and Jeffrey's phonics and—"

"No, no," I shook my head and waved my hands. "I have enough information."

She smiled in approval.

"You know," I said, "you're a good teacher."

"I know I *want* to be a good teacher. Like I said, it looks good on paper. I need to stay disciplined to adhere to the lesson plans. If I do that, it'll be a good *academic* year."

"Academic," I repeated, to assure her I caught the emphasis in her voice.

"Yes, remember, there's more to home-schooling than academics. It's total education."

My lips mouthed the words as she said them. Slowly, I was starting to get on board with Union Station Education.

Home-School Trivial Pursuit came to a close with all questions answered. Somewhere between the trivial and the technical was the stuff my friends called "nuts and bolts."

Rhonda was helping me discover that *home-schooling* is a term of delicate balance. Yes, it's *schooling,* but it's more than just academics transferred to a home setting. It's *home.* Real, live, family living. Academics are important, but only as one aspect of what I was learning to call *total education.*

Academics had to be seen as one piece of the Home-School Trivial Pursuit Pie.

4

Return to Walton's Mountain

Morning chores.

Those two words always conjure up warm thoughts of America gone by. It's the feelings that come from waking up early, milking the cows, slopping the hogs, gathering the eggs, feeding the sheep, and grooming the horses—all before breakfast.

I know what you're thinking. High tech is in vogue today. Morning chores are more like checking over the hard copy of the overnight printouts made available through your modem interfacing with your megabyte.

Well, for those of you who think that morning chores are a thing of the past, I've got a way for you to turn back the hands of time: Morning Chores are a top priority in the curriculum provided in Union Station Education. We even have our own version of John-Boy, Jim-Bob, and all the gang on Walton's Mountain.

Back in the early days of our home-schooling, Rhonda felt the need to explain her philosophy as she went along. It was kind of a parenting play-by-play.

"Home-schooling is much more than academics," she began one morning. "Listen to this portion of a marvelous book I'm reading." I looked at the cover and saw the title *For the Children's Sake* by Susan Schaeffer Macaulay. Rhonda began to read:

> When a baby is picked up, spoken to, and loved, he is starting his education as God planned it. For all our lives we are human beings, in an active state of learning, responding, understanding. Education extends to all of life. In fact an educational system that says that one bright summer's day in the dawn of my youth, "There; now you are educated. This piece of paper says so," is doing me a gross disfavor. The truly educated person has only had many doors of interest opened. He knows that life will not be long enough to follow everything through fully.

Rhonda sighed and put the book down. "That's what I want for our kids—education *in total*." She emphasized the last two words.

"In total," I repeated.

"Yes, in total," she continued. "And what is more real to living than the everyday necessities of life?"

"You mean eating and sleeping?" I asked. "That's great! I'd give every one of our kids an *A* in those subjects . . . and I'd give myself an *A*-plus!"

Rhonda put her hands on her hips and frowned. "Bill, I'm not talking about those kinds of necessities. I'm talking about necessities around the house. Things like cleaning their rooms and taking out the trash, doing dishes, and learning to do their own laundry."

It was the last chore that caught my attention. If there was one thing we had learned by having lots of kids, it was this: You'll *never* do away with Mount Saint Dirty Clothes. I can't tell you how many times I've said to Rhonda, "Why do you do so much laundry?" And in the true mountaineer spirit she's always replied, "Because it's there."

I began to get excited about this whole project of "total education." *And why not?* I thought. *How many times did I help clean chalkboards or bang erasers or put chairs up on desks when I was in school? I could've used that energy to clean my own clothes!* That really hit home. "I cleaned a lot of chalkboards in fifth grade," I mused. "And I dirtied a lot of clothes."

I have to confess, I never learned how to do my own laundry until I was eighteen and moved away to college. The guys in the men's dorm gave me simple instructions:

1. *Wait until* everything *you own is dirty beyond recognition.*
2. *Hermetically seal the laundry in an airtight bag.*
3. *Enter the college Laundromat, preferably right before going to work.*
4. *Look for a girl.*
5. *Display the saddest, sorriest look known to man.*
6. *When a girl comes to inquire about the sadness, explain to her how you were up all last night helping your little sister over her junior-high boyfriend problems. Now you're supposed to be at work, and yet you'll risk losing your job in order to wear clean clothes.*
7. *Pick up your clean laundry at a predetermined spot after work.*

So, to think that my kids could handle their own Mount Saint Dirty Clothes was an exciting prospect indeed!

Morning chores caught on quickly at our place. Most of the items had already been in motion. Cleaning your room, taking out the trash, doing dishes, and cleaning up dog doo-doo were tasks that were accomplished throughout the day. We simply changed some of the timing to get the kids into a morning groove.

But the washing machine was a new venture. About the only time the kids had seen the washer up close was when the old bucket-of-bolts took sick and started walking through the house. I was fortunate enough to be home the day they met for real.

My mind raced back to the words of Dr. Moore concerning the value of chores. *It's good for their self-esteem, it's good for camaraderie, it's good for teaching them the things traditionally associated only with formal schooling,* I thought. "Plus, it gets our clothes clean!" I said aloud.

We all jammed into our tiny laundry room. One half of the entire room was occupied by the washer and dryer. The other half of the room was shelves with soap, bleach, fabric softener, lint resisters, Cling-Free tosses, and every other imaginable laundry convenience. The center of the room was reserved for the dirty clothes.

Rumor has it the walls of the laundry room are a light blue, but no one in our family has actually seen the walls.

"Kids, this is our washing machine and this is our dryer," Rhonda announced in much the same way a museum tour guide points out the brontosaurus and the Tyrannosaurus rex. "I'd like you to go to your rooms, get your dirty clothes, and meet me back here in the laundry room."

As they went off to their rooms, there was an excitement in their eyes. *The pioneers climbed many a mountain such as this,* I thought. I suddenly realized that I was slowly but steadily becoming a convert to Pioneer Spirit.

By now some of you think I'm exaggerating in describing our laundry as Mount Saint Dirty Clothes. *Some* of you think I'm exaggerating; the rest of you are parents. You know far too well how much clothing two adults and four children can "sweat out," "muddy up," or "soil," depending on the age and gender of the family member.

As the mountain moved to the laundry room, it became quickly apparent that this was one morning chore that would extend deep into the afternoon and evening.

Rhonda announced the schedule. "Jesse-Boy, you'll do your wash on Mondays, Tuesdays will be Jeffrey-Bob, Wednesdays will be for Joy-Lynna-Ma-Ka-Bob, and I'll do Baby Johnny-Ju-Ju-Bee-Boy's on Thursdays."

"I'll do my laundry on Friday nights before I go on my weekend speaking trips," I said to everyone, in total make-believe.

"Wonderful, wonderful," Rhonda beamed. "That's the spirit! What do you think of your dad, kids?"

The kids all cheered, clapped, and clomped.

"But I was only kid—"

"Now, now, not another word." Rhonda wagged her index finger and effectively signed me up for a Friday-night function I failed to find fulfilling.

Rhonda quickly turned her attention to her pursuit for the day: Understanding the Washing Machine's Temperament. She gathered all of us around the square, white, metal visual aid.

"See this knob here?" she asked.

"Yeah."

"Yeah."

"Yeah."

"Yeah."

All eyes stared at me.

"DAD!" yelled all four.

"Yeah," I said, feeling embarrassed to have missed the cue.

"This is the temperature control. Turn it this way, it's hot; turn it the other way, it's cold; leave it in the middle, it's warm."

"Mom, do you use a 'tergent for each different tempercher, or do you use the same one for all three?" It was Jeffrey-Bob, obviously imitating a television commercial.

"That's a good question, Jeffrey," stated Rhonda with way too much patience, as far as I was concerned. "We use the one detergent for all temperatures."

Everyone seemed pleased with that answer. I smiled, giving in to peer pressure.

"Divide your laundry into two piles," Rhonda continued her lesson. "Put all your whites in one pile and all your colors in the other." The kids cooperated quite nicely and did just that.

"The whites can be washed in hot water. Things like underwear, T-shirts, white socks, and towels can get good and clean in the hot water."

The kids were still with Rhonda, following along with every word.

"The colors are washed in cold water. If you did them in hot, the colors would all run together and it would be a real mess."

Jesse-Boy turned to me and mocked, "Remember that, Dad. Please don't wash your colors in hot."

I nodded to him, acknowledging his taunt, but nonetheless making a mental note of that important factor in washing machine usage.

"Now, put a load of clothes in up to about here." Rhonda pointed to a line in the basin. "Take the cap off the container of liquid detergent, pour the soap into the cap, pour the cap over the clothes, close the lid, and pull this knob." As she pulled it out, we all heard the water beginning to fill the tank.

So we started whittling away at the mountain, one load at a time. About every forty-five minutes another child would get a chance at starting his or her own load of clothes. I had never seen laundry bring such pleasure to little people. They were learning a new concept, mastering that concept, and experiencing the confidence and pleasure that comes from that mastery.

The only person experiencing more pleasure than the kids was their new teacher. I leaned over, kissed her on the cheek, and whispered in her ear, "If you're as good at phonics and math as you are at colors and whites, our kids have got it made!"

She squeezed me back and whispered, "If that's the way you really feel, I'll make you a little deal!"

My ears perked up. "Go right ahead, superteacher, I'm listening!"

"Well, I'll continue to do your laundry if you keep telling me how I'm doing," she went on. "I want you to be loving, yet very honest with me."

I pulled away from the hug to look her straight in the eye. "You're serious, aren't you?" I asked.

"Yes, Bill, I really am serious." Her eyes started filling up. "I'm a strong woman with lots of determination and all that pioneer spirit you're always making fun of," she continued. "But the fact is, I get sorta scared of all this at times. It's such a heavy responsibility. I guess I'm just saying that your encouragement would mean a lot more to me than wiping out a pile of dirty laundry."

I responded, "I know I kid you a lot, babe, but I want you to know that being an encouragement to you is about the easiest assignment a teacher could give a guy. I'll support you in this new venture, because I'm beginning to see how good it is and because I love you more than anything in this world."

Two misty-eyed parents embraced once again. It was a

long, tender embrace. It would have been longer, but Joy came back in and mangled the moment by announcing, "You two are hugging over my pile of colors." So much for love in the laundry room.

So if we left it at that, you'd conclude that the kids did their own laundry and I never did mine. That is true, but I want to add that I was once called upon in a consultant status to analyze washing machine malfunction. In other words, the night the dumb washer broke, I had to try and fix it.

By a strange twist of fate, the washer ceased functioning on a Friday evening. And it just so happened to have a load of *my* clothing in its tummy. And I did need them for a weekend speaking trip. So when I heard the machine making a sound much like the mating call of a Tibetan yak, I covered my ears for protection and moved toward the noisemaker.

Since the washer had a history of moving around on its own, we had placed it on another wall of the laundry room, right next to the dryer. When I say "right next to" the dryer, I mean that the wall was wide enough for only one washer and one dryer. Not an inch to spare. Not half an inch to spare. They were tighter than Siamese twins.

I arrived at the scene just in time to witness its expiration. Yes, it died right there in my arms. I quickly opened the lid to discover one of the most depressing laws of nature known to man: A washing machine will never conk out in the spin cycle. It will always die in the wash cycle.

Of course, this means that there are gallons upon gallons of water that remain in the tub of the machine.

All the guts of the machine are in the back. So now I've got a dead washer, full of water, jammed up tightly next to the dryer on one side and a wall on the other. It was Moses and the Red Sea all over again.

I determined I would be unable to move the machine to get to the back of it in its present condition. I rolled up my sleeves, grabbed a bucket, and started to bail. The bucket was a good idea, but it was too big to get down into the tub because of the agitator in the middle.

"Now I know where you got your name," I mumbled as I hit the agitator with my fist.

So I had to improvise. I found a pitcher in the kitchen that looked to be the right dimensions. It was close, but still too big to fit in a circular tub.

I had no other choice. I was forced to bail with a plastic Scooby Doo drinking glass.

I looked at my watch. *I have a plane to catch in twelve hours,* I thought. *At this rate, I'll never make it.*

It was then that I had a joyful recollection. "We have a service maintenance agreement on this little baby!" I was ecstatic with gladness and relief.

I ran back to our bedroom and quickly found the maintenance agreement in our file cabinet. I had it filed between the electric bills and the water bills, since a washing machine needed both to operate.

I skipped to the phone, dialed the number, listened to the ring, heard a voice, began explaining my problem, only to hear music.

Apparently I had been speaking with a tape which informed me that I would be on hold until they worked their way through the calls preceding me. "Please relax, be patient, and enjoy the same music you hear in the dentist's waiting room while waiting for your root canal."

I sat, squirmed, and shuffled until finally humanity broke through. "This is Ms. Munson. May I help you?"

"Ah yes, thank the Lord for real people!" I exclaimed. "You see, it's my washing machine. It just died."

"Do you have a service contract?"

"Yes."

"Contract number?"

"B6284GFL17843XL283366BGY."

"No, that's the washer ID number. I need the service contract number in the upper left-hand corner of your agreement card."

"Oh, I see it—18966."

"Thank you. Washer ID number?"

"The long one I just gave you?"

"Yes."

"I just gave it to you!!"

"I'll need it again, sir."

"B6284GFL17843XL283366BGY."

"Thank you."

I heard the computer grunting as I was groaning.

"I have good news, Mr. Butterworm," she said.

"That's Butter*worth,*" I corrected.

"No, according to our records, it's Butterworm."

I resisted the urge to clarify her records. "Well, anyway, what's the good news?"

"Your service contract is in operation, so we'll send our first available man to your home."

"That's wonderful!" I applauded.

"Our first available man will be in your area next Thursday."

"THURSDAY! THAT'S SIX DAYS AWAY!!"

"Yes, sir, that is correct."

"But my clothes are in the machine right now and I

have to go on a business trip tomorrow morning IN THOSE CLOTHES!"

"Well, in that case, I suggest you call this 800-number for the nearest parts store in your area. You'll need to fix the machine yourself: 1-800-555-6870."

So, when I say I tried to fix our washer that fateful Friday night, I really mean:

1. *I bailed.*
2. *I called my friend Wayne, who can fix everything.*
3. *I handed Wayne the tools he needed. (I don't know them by name; he had to point them out for me.)*
4. *I fed Wayne lotsa cookies and coffee.*
5. *We talked about the Rams, the Raiders, and Lyle Alzado.*
6. *I helped Wayne carry his tools back out to his car.*

I left town that weekend with clean clothes and no sleep.

As I was returning home on the plane that following Sunday night, I thought a great deal about our legacy in the laundry room. Here I was, a grown man, just beginning to see what dirty clothes and dippy washers were all about.

But my children are learning the ins and outs of this everyday stuff at their young age. Yes, this total education was scoring big points with me. I was pleased to be a parent in a home where morning chores still had the old-fashioned meaning.

I glanced at my watch. It was 9:00 P.M. I could just hear my crew now, even though I was still far away.

"Good night, Jeffrey-Bob."

"Good night, Jesse-Boy."

"Good night, Mama."

"Good night, Joy-Lynna-Ma-Ka-Bob."

"Good night, Johnny-Ju-Ju-Bee-Boy."

(Lights go out one by one, bring up closing theme song and credits.)

"Rest well," I mumbled from my seat in the plane. "For tomorrow begins another week of total education . . . and morning chores."

5

George Washington Had a Tutor

Morning chores soon became a real test of character. Could four home-educated young ones take full responsibility for their assigned tasks? Could they do so without constant adult supervision? What happened to the motivator of morning chores, anyway?

Mrs. Morning Chore became Mrs. Morning Sick.

That's correct. No sooner had we lined up the whole morning schedule of tasks when we realized Mama was pregnant.

Again.

That was the operative answer as we shared the news of the Butter Number Five:

"Again?"

"Again!"

"Aga, aga, aga. . . ."

Everyone had his own variation. But despite their surprise, Rhonda and I knew what we were doing and it was good news. But it did change some things.

The term *morning sickness* is really a misnomer at our house. In actuality, morning sickness is a daily early hour routine that precedes *afternoon sickness,* which is followed by *evening sickness,* concluded by *it's-too-uncomfortable-for-sleeping sickness.*

This cycle of discomfort lasts three days short of nine months. The three days are: 1. the day the pregnancy is discovered, 2. the day you hear the baby's heartbeat for the first time, and 3. the day the baby is delivered. The first two days are too joyous to be sick. The last day is too agonizing to be referred to simply as sickness.

The big question on everyone's mind was, What will this pregnancy do to home-education at Union Station?

"I guess the kids will have to go back to school," I muttered to myself with a real mixed reaction.

"Joy, this means we'll have a nine-month summer vacation," Jesse whispered to his sister.

"No, Jesse," Joy replied matter-of-factly. "This means I'll teach you and you'll teach me." Leave it to Joy to get creative.

"It doesn't mean any of that stuff," came the voice of a woman eating crackers in bed. "I'll keep teaching you guys at home. I can do it. I just know I can. But we'll have to modify a little. We might need to put Heppie Bread on the back burner for now."

I raised my eyebrows in silent disbelief. I knew my wife was strong. And I knew my wife was determined. But I also knew that pregnancies were tough on this little gal. She had courage, but I wondered if she could really pull off the whole home scene with the only sacrifice being Heppie Bread.

Morning chores became a matter of personal integrity. Mama was no longer right behind to check up on the busy hands at work. But it was heartwarming to see those industrious little students dig right in and clean that room, feed that dog, do that laundry, tote that barge, and lift that bale.

Rhonda had already developed a daily routine that called for the academic side of the schooling to take place after lunch, while John napped. Of course, John often snuck back out and eavesdropped on school—to Mama's delight. More often than not, those afternoon hours were the strongest and healthiest hours for Rhonda. Thus the teaching went on, relatively uninterrupted.

The study of history became the favorite subject in Union Station Education. We decided to zero in on United States history and, in particular, the presidents of the United States.

"Why don't we spend one week on each president of the United States?" Rhonda proposed. "And if it takes longer than a week, we can spill over into the next one. But basically, we should be able to cover all of them in a year."

That's one of the advantages of teaching your own kids and developing your own curriculum—flexibility. If Abraham Lincoln takes two weeks and Millard Fillmore takes two days, that's just fine. If one child goes crazy with interest over FDR but is bored to tears with Calvin Coolidge, great! Simply flex. I realize classroom teachers do the same thing, but flexing for two is much easier than flexing for twenty-eight.

The first stages of preparation included taking inventory of available resources. I found a book on the presidents I had as a child. "It only goes up to Eisenhower, but it'll help us with most of them," I quipped.

Rhonda visited the local bookstore and found a book she knew the kids would love. It was a real find. The book was about two-feet high by one-foot wide. It contained a full-color portrait of each president on the right-hand page and a brief biography and list of facts on the left-hand page. Visuals are really very important to kids and the ability to stare face-to-face at Andrew Jackson was vital.

"And it was on the sale table!" shouted Rhonda with an excitement she knew I would share.

"I'm traveling to Washington, D.C., in a couple of months," I volunteered. "I'm sure I can pick up something on the presidents at the Smithsonian Institution!"

The kids were absolutely beside themselves with excitement. Mama and Daddy were going bonkers over Chester Arthur and it was contagious.

We went to the library and checked out books on Washington, Adams, and Jefferson. Some were kids' books they could read themselves; others were advanced and had to be read to them. Still others were for parents to read and then translate for their youngsters.

Rhonda and I became wacko over Washington trivia.

"Did you know that George Washington was really born on February 11, not February 22?" I asked one day.

"Yes, that's because the British Parliament discarded the Julian calendar in 1750 and adopted the Gregorian calendar. In 1753 they added eleven days to the calendar, thus putting Washington's birthday at the traditional February 22 date." Rhonda was well informed. I was impressed. The kids were loving it.

"How about this one?" continued my lovely home-schooling historian. "Although George Washington was one of the richest men of his time, he was 'land-poor' and had to borrow money to go to his first inauguration!"

But it was an innocent little fact concerning the schooling of the father of our country that became the motto of our mission.

"Did you know," Rhonda continued, "when George Washington was a little boy, he had a tutor?"

Apparently the kids had never heard the word *tutor* before. By the looks on their faces, this word was coming across to them as somewhere between the sound of a whistle and a make-believe word a baby would use when he wants his teddy bear.

Well, Rhonda said the word and the kids burst out laughing on cue and in unison. They got sillier and sillier.

"George Washington had a . . . had a . . . had a TUTOR!" Joy giggled.

"George Washington had a toot-toot!" snickered Jesse.

"George Washington had a tootsie!" mocked Jeffrey.

"George Washington had a tutu!" smiled John.

We all joined in the silliness and giggled right along with them. Once it settled down, Rhonda capitalized on the teachable moment. "Do any of you know what a tutor really is?"

They all shook their heads.

"A tutor is someone who teaches. Most tutors teach students one at a time. George Washington probably had a tutor who taught him right in his house."

"Like us?" asked Joy.

"Yes, it's very similar to what we're doing," replied Rhonda.

"And you're our tutor, right, Mom?" piped in Jesse.

"That's right!" Rhonda answered.

You could feel the sense of pride enter the room. In a very tiny way, they were reaching out and touching the past. They were relating history to their home. George

Washington's tutor was being replaced by a significant other . . . Mama.

My main contribution to the children's tutor was to keep her well stocked with her most current craving resulting from her pregnancy. To a novice this may sound like a simple assignment, but to any man who's lived with a pregnant woman, the complication is clear.

"Honey, I'm just too sick to face the prospect of fixing a meal for all of us," Rhonda would say, in one of our typical late-afternoon phone conversations.

"Hey, that's all right," I'd begin in understanding tones. "I'll either fix something or run out to get something."

"Ah, you're so sweet. I sure do love you."

"I love you too," I assured. "Now, what would you like for dinner?"

"Weell . . ." she'd start off slowly. "If you really want to know, I do have a sorta craving right now."

I never understood what a "sorta craving" was, but I realized I was about to pass the point of no return.

"Sure, I really want to know. What is it that you're sorta craving?"

"Chinese food" was the object of her desire.

"Great!" I exclaimed. "I can stop by the China Garden on my way home from work. It's right on the way, so it won't be any trouble at all!" I felt good being such a real need-meeter, yet not having to go to the other side of town in order to do so.

"Sweetie?" Rhonda asked with a tentative voice.

"Yes?" I responded with equal reluctance.

"I really like the egg drop soup, chicken chow mein, egg roll, and barbecue pork ribs that we get when we go to the Mandarin Pavilion."

"No problem," I countered. "I'm sure they have all of those items at China Garden."

"But I especially like the way they make it at Mandarin Pavilion."

"But that restaurant is clear over on the other side of town!" I protested.

Silence.

"Well, you did ask what I was craving, so I told you. You go wherever you think is best."

Now, what's a guy to do, folks?

The terrific tutor of Union Station Education was down for the count with a terrible bout of pregnancy. I could be practical, cost-effective, and time-efficient by buying dinner at the China Garden or I could be impractical, overbudget, and wastefully inefficient by making the journey to Mandarin Pavilion.

I finally decided on the latter. After all, what good is it to be practical, cost-effective, and efficient while you're sleeping on the couch?

Since this was pregnancy number five, I knew Mandarin Pavilion was just the beginning of the long list of delicacies known as Rhonda's Cravings.

The next night Chinese food had been abandoned for a less substantial item—Doritos. So it was a quick stop by our grocery store on the way home from work to pick up a giant-size bag of Pre-natal Nummy Nums.

However, by the time I arrived home with the Doritos, the kids had an important announcement. "Mama's changed her mind! She doesn't want yukky old Doritos, she wants yummy, yummy Oreo cookies!"

"Daddy, I'll go back to the store with you." Joy volunteered. "I know right where the Oreos are, too, so I can be a big help!"

"Okay, you can ride down with me," I agreed with some discomfort. The discomfort came from knowing that inviting one kid to the store was really inviting four. So they all piled in the car.

As we rode down the block, I quietly listened in as the kids discussed the most pressing subject on their minds: Would President Reagan eat Oreos?

Jeffrey concluded he wouldn't because old people don't eat fun food.

Joy countered by saying that old people *do* eat fun food, or else we wouldn't be going to the store right now to buy Oreos for Mama.

Jesse felt that President Reagan would eat Oreos, " 'cause I like President Reagan and I like Oreos."

John didn't care, as long as President Reagan didn't eat Oreos that belonged to John.

We parked the car, unloaded the troops, ran to the cookie aisle, grabbed a large bag of the good stuff, and stood in line at the checkout counter. When we got to the checker, she began to make small talk with the kids.

"Ah-ha, it looks like somebody likes Oreo cookies!"

"Yes, President Reagan," quipped Jesse as all the kids giggled.

"I see," smiled our conversational checker. "Are you guys experts on the presidents?"

The timing was perfect. I couldn't resist. "Hit it, kids," I announced.

Jesse began, "Did you know that John Adams ran for president against Thomas Jefferson, and when Adams won, since Jefferson came in second, he became the vice-president?"

The checker looked stunned, as I nodded in proud approval. "That's the old Pioneer Spirit!"

Joy piped in, "James Madison was the only president to face enemy gunfire while in office."

"Thank you, Joy," I beamed. It was now Jeffrey's turn.

"The 'nited States got twice as big when Thomas Jefferson was president, 'cause he bought Louisiana."

As the checker dropped her jaw, I translated, "The Louisiana Purchase."

John settled on the most significant historical fact he had learned in quite a few weeks. "Did you know that when George Washington was a little boy"—he paused for effect—"HE HAD A TUTOR!"

All four kids roared with laughter and old Dad joined right in. We left the poor little checker in a state of shock.

Boy, she sure got more than she bargained for, I thought as we walked out of the store with our reward: Oreos.

The reason I call it "our reward" is that by the time we got back home, Rhonda had changed her craving again.

I was met at the door with "I sure could go for some fresh honey-wheat doughnuts from the Doughnut Shop." Like I said, Oreos were *our* reward.

And the term *reward* is really quite appropriate, I think. Our kids were more excited about history than at any other time in their history. From my point of view, excitement is half the battle in education. If students become motivated about a particular subject, they'll do whatever it takes to gain mastery of that subject. It was obvious to me that we had four cases of terminal presidential excitement. Add Mama and Dad's pleasure and you have one fine house of history.

There's an old rule of education that goes something like this: Success leads to success. We were all mastering simple, succinct facts about George Washington and that was the success we needed to become excited over John Adams. And the mastery of the Adams administration opened up to the world of Jefferson. It was the domino effect alive and well at Union Station. All the way down to the Doughnut Shop and back I was beaming from ear to ear—proud to be an American, proud to be a parent (I swallowed hard). Was I becoming proud of being a home-school parent?

So when I finally arrived home with the fresh honey-wheat doughnuts only to find Rhonda eating an apple, I realized that her cravings contributed to the process of presidential review, but all these trips to the store would soon wear me out.

What I didn't realize was the apple in Rhonda's hand would soon be symbolizing the most exciting aspect of Union Station Education I would experience as a parent.

6

Aaa, Aaa, Apple
for the
Teacher

I was trying as hard as I could to be a helper and an encourager to my pretty pregnant pedagogue. For all the weight I'd lose running to markets and restaurants for items of desire, I'd gain it all back (and more) by joining right in and eating those treats.

In other words, using pregnant lingo, I was starting to show.

"They need to make maternity clothes for men!" I griped one morning as I struggled to fit into my clothes. I stared jealously at Rhonda's new outfits, complete with lots of additional material and inches and inches of extra elastic.

"Don't be silly," Rhonda taunted. "Men don't get pregnant!"

Her verbal jab hurt me in the pit of my stomach.

"Oh yeah?" I responded. "Well, for your information, I think I just felt the baby kick!"

I walked out of the bedroom and into the kitchen. Our kitchen is basic butcher block and Butterworth. The contrast between the butcher-block counter and the white cabinets was obvious. The kids tended to camouflage crumbs on the butcher block, but peanut butter was painfully noticeable on white cabinet doors.

It's your typical kitchen with stove, oven, sink, and refrigerator. Like most refrigerators in the U S of A, ours is a showplace for meaningful memories. Little colorful magnets hold up pictures, newspaper clippings, and Mama's favorite mementos: *Family Circus* cartoons she has collected down through the years. (Rhonda swears Bil Keane has direct access to our house!)

The walls are white for now. We'll redo it in fun colors when our redecorating ship comes in. At this rate the kids may be adults before that ship arrives, but that could be good timing. Kids would only destroy the remodeling, anyway, right?

Well, life had begun in the kitchen about ten minutes before I arrived. The kids were fixing themselves breakfast.

This sight was both gratifying and painful. Joy was fixing instant oatmeal for herself and John. She poured the oats in her bowl and mixed in hot water. However, for John's oatmeal the oats were added to the water so they would sorta float on top. Don't ask me why, but that's the way he always has his oatmeal. I guess he always will. I know—I made it the other way *once*. "Wet oakmilk is yukky," was his pronouncement.

Jeffrey was pouring cold cereal into a bowl. Perhaps it would be more accurate to say he was *attempting* to pour cold cereal into a bowl. Most of it was escaping the bowl and making a run for it down the kitchen counter. As he reached for the gallon of milk, I held my breath. Fortunately, it was one of his luckier moments. He did get some milk in the bowl on the first try.

The real action was over by the toaster. Jesse was creating a culinary delight with toast, peanut butter, and jelly. This is quite a scary sight as everything in the close proximity of the toaster is a sickening brownish purple with bumps. Jesse is one of those kids who demonstrates his concentration by sticking out his tongue and placing it up on his upper lip. I could tell there was a high degree of difficulty in spreading the jelly because his tongue was resting on his nose.

"Need some help, Jess?" I asked.

"No, I've got it, Dad," came the confident reply. "Anyway, Jeffrey has kitchen cleanup, so he'll be wiping up this mess in just a few minutes."

"No, he's not cleaning up—I am!" It was Joy, Mama's little helper, coming to the rescue of a brother in need. "Jeffrey's gonna do his other chores, but he needs to get ready 'cause Mama's gonna teach him how to read today!"

Two big eyes grew even bigger from behind Cold Cereal Canyon. "Do you really mean it, Joy?" he asked. "Is Mama really gonna teach me to read?"

"Yup," she replied. "All she was waiting for was the cricklum to come in and it was in yesterday's mail."

The cricklum. I smiled. We were all quite excited over the arrival of Jeffrey's studies. We had chosen the curriculum provided by the Calvert School in Baltimore, Maryland, as the overall course of study for our little guy. They've been at the business of writing home-instruction courses for decades. They came highly recommended by educators and we were anxious to dive in headfirst.

For reading, we were also made aware of a marvelous program called *Sing, Spell, Read, and Write* from CBN Center in Virginia Beach, Virginia. It's a total language-arts program for grades kindergarten through third. Phonics, reading, spelling, writing, and speaking are all addressed.

Meanwhile my Joy was still discussing the "cricklum."

"The *curriculum*," I corrected. But my correction wasn't heard. I didn't press because the distraction was a messy kitchen counter. How could I interrupt this labor of love? There's my little princess, grunting over a chore that isn't even hers. Yet she's doing it so that her little brother can get all ready to learn his letters, phonics, and blends. Union Station Education was sure producing some team spirit. And it sure made me proud to be a part of it.

I left for work that morning knowing that this was going to be a special day for a special guy.

It would be exciting for us as parents too! Joy and Jesse had attended school previously, and both of them began home-schooling already knowing how to read. Jeffrey was our first opportunity to start at the beginning.

Pride was welling up inside me as I could hear people saying, "My, my, this little boy reads very well for his age." And I could see Jeffrey, beaming from ear to ear, saying, "My mama taught me how to read! She's the greatest!"

Admittedly, I was doing a great deal of clock watching that day. Around one o'clock that afternoon I thought, *They're starting. This is it! Our own personal war against illiteracy!*

My excitement came to a screeching halt with a phone call at 1:15.

"Daddy?" On the other end of the line was the voice of a little guy fighting back the tears.

"Jeffrey, is that you?"

"It's not fair, Daddy, it's just not fair!" Jeffrey began sobbing, totally out of control. I wasn't sure what was happening, but it was breaking his little heart.

"What is it, son? What's wrong?" I tried to be as calm as possible.

"I'm not (sob, heave, sigh) gonna learn (more sob, heave, sigh) how to—to—to read today." He blurted out the last three words and then lost it again—in full force.

"Why not, buddy?"

As I asked, I heard the phone drop to the floor. I heard some scrambling for it, and the voice on the line told me that Joy had come on to fill me in on the details.

"Joy, what's going on? Why is Jeffrey so upset?"

"It's Mama," Joy explained. "She's having another one of those days!"

"You mean?"

"Yup. She's gonna be morning sick all day."

"So she won't be able to teach Jeffrey today," I concluded. "No wonder he's so hurt. He's been looking forward to this for such a long time."

My mind flashed back to some of our trips to the public library. Joy and Jesse would excitedly browse through the first- and second-grade sections, finding fun books like *Nate the Great, Amelia Bedelia,* and *Pippi Longstocking*. They'd bring them home and read them all by themselves. Oftentimes, right before bedtime, Jeffrey would lay down in Jesse's bed and John would crawl in with Joy and the older would read to the younger, to the delight of everyone involved.

But that delight was dimming as Jeffrey continued to grow. He really wanted to read for himself. He wanted to go to the same library shelves his older brother and sister frequented.

I tried to get Jeffrey back on the phone, but he had run off to his room to fully vent his emotions. I put in the longest afternoon of my career and headed home for some high-powered cheerleading.

When I walked in the front door, I discovered another poor soul I had overlooked in the whole incident—Rhonda.

My sweetie was lying on the couch, reading through Jeffrey's new curriculum, groaning in obvious discomfort from 5:00 P.M. morning sickness.

"You don't love me? You don't care?"

Rhonda says that in a silly French accent. Over the years of our marriage, this had come to be a coded message. Once I broke the code, I discovered it is her way of saying, "You didn't call me on the phone from the office this afternoon."

It always means trouble, too.

"Yes, I love you, and yes, I care," I responded as I bent down and kissed her on the forehead. "I hear you've had a really rough day."

"True, it's been a killer," she replied. "But have you heard about Jeffrey?"

"He called me at work early this afternoon. He's really crushed. What can we do to cheer him up?"

"Well, the kids are all complaining because when I have these days *you* have to cook."

"They're complaining about that!"

"Well, Bill, you'll have to admit, we're all getting a little tired of you 'cooking' peanut butter and jelly every night."

This statement was a real bruise to my ego, but I attempted to continue. "Okay, how about if I *really* cook a meal tonight? Maybe that will cheer him up."

"We do have the stuff to make spaghetti in the kitchen already," she added. "I'm sorta craving Italian tonight, anyway."

I knocked on Jeffrey's bedroom door and was greeted with gloom. "Hi, Dad," came a voice that was void of energy. "I didn't learn to read today."

"I know," I assured him as I lifted him up onto my lap. "Mama's been morning sick all day, so I've gotta go cook dinner now."

Jeffrey fell right into my trap. He had that "Oh, no, not peanut butter and jelly again" look all over his face.

"But let's not have peanut butter and jelly tonight," I went on. "Let's have some food that's *really* cooked."

His eyes began to flicker the tiniest little bit.

"How about spaghetti, Jeffrey?"

"Pasketti?" His eyes were like saucers. "Really? Do you mean it?"

"Sure! Mama's gonna give me step-by-step instructions. It'll be easy!"

The two of us marched, skipped, and hopped into the kitchen, and Morning-Sick Mama did play-by-play for the Spaghetti Bowl.

"Brown the meat."

"Check!"

"Drain the grease."

"Right."

"Drain it into the small can under the sink. Don't put it anywhere else."

"Oh!"

"Pour the sauce into the pan with the meat."

"Check."

"Start boiling water in the big pan!"

"Boiling water? Is it time? Are you going to deliver right here at the house?" I couldn't resist having fun with my cutie.

"Very funny," she mocked, but you know as well as I do by now, she loved it.

"What's next?" I asked.

"Pour the spaghetti into the boiling water."

"Righto!"

"Now wait a little, then drain the spaghetti by putting it in the colander."

"Okay."

"Set the table and we're ready to eat."

Thus came the first actual meal "cooked" by a novice such as I. It wasn't all that great, but it was better than peanut butter and jelly, so it went over very big.

After dinner it was clean up, wrestle, bathe, pajama, and hit the sack. As the kids prayed that night, all of them asked God to help Mama feel better tomorrow. And we all knew the request was for more than just one woman's health.

Well, God graciously answered the fervent prayers of four little children. The next day, morning sickness was confined to the morning.

Afternoon arrived and one excited student named Jeffrey Eugene Butterworth sat down at his place at our dining room table. And he wasn't there to eat!

Learning the sounds of the letters was the first order of business. Jeffrey's introduction to reading was in the shape of a giant piece of fruit covering page 1 in his workbook.

"What is in this picture, Jeffrey?" asked Rhonda.

"It's an apple, Mama," replied a child who could hardly contain himself.

"That's correct. Now, say it again, but this time say it real slow."

"Aaaaple."

"Very good! Now just say the first part of the word, okay?"

"Aaa."

"Again."

"Aaa."

"Great! Now, let's put it together and say 'Aaa, aaa, apple.' "

"Aaa, aaa, apple."

"Wonderful! Now let's hear it again."

"Aaa, aaa, apple!" The excitement in his little voice was overwhelming.

"Jeffrey, that's wonderful!" Rhonda was equal to him in exhilaration. "Now let's listen to this cassette tape. It has a song about each of the letters, and it starts out with the one you learned today!"

"You mean aaa, aaa, apple?"

"Yes, I do. Listen."

The tape was a song that presented the alphabet in a clever lyric:

> "Aaa, aaa, apple, bh, bh, ball
> Ck, ck, cat, and dh, dh, doll
> Eh, eh, egg, and fff, fff, fan
> Ggh, ggh, goat, and hhh, hhh, hand."

I'll have to admit it was a catchy little tune and, without question, Jeffrey loved it.

But music tends to draw a crowd at our place. After the tape had played for only a few seconds, Joy, Jesse, and John all found their way to the dining room to enjoy the song as well.

Union Station was absolutely buzzing by the time I arrived home that evening. Jeffrey met me at the door with his usual hug and kiss, and then he promptly escorted me to the west wall of the dining room.

"Isn't it beautiful, Dad?" asked an obviously proud student of letters. There on the wall was an eight-by-eleven-inch picture of an apple, carefully colored in with red crayon. Rhonda had removed it from the workbook and taped it to the pine paneling.

Jeffrey continued to stare at it, almost in a trance.

"It's an apple," I announced, breaking the silence.

"Not just any old apple, Dad," I was quickly corrected. "This is aaa, aaa, apple."

"Jeffrey, that's wonderful!"

"And do you know what else, Dad?"

"What?"

"The next time we have school we'll do bh, bh, ball. Mama says we can do a new letter every day until we get to zz, zz, zoo! And I get to put the pitchers I color up on the wall and it'll be filled with all my stuff and before too long I'll be putting them all together and I'll be reading and we can go to the library and I'll be able to pick out books that I can read all by myself and then I'll—"

"Wow!" I had to interrupt. He was about to blow a gasket and I felt it was necessary to get him back to a safe fifty-five miles per hour. "It sounds to me like you're going to be a reader real soon!"

"That's right, Dad. I'll be able to read to you guys all the stories you and Mama have read to me!"

"Well, Jeffrey, that's terrific."

"I'll read you *Winnie the Pooh* and *Charlotte's Web,* and *Stuart Little* and, and . . . I'll even read you the books you write!"

Needless to say, the dinner that evening was like a day at Disneyland. Jeffrey could hardly eat. He was a compact, nonstop talking machine, telling all of us over and over how he was going to read every book ever written.

Now I must admit, there were days when his excitement was wearying. But overall, this was one of the most exciting aspects of home-education I have been able to observe. As the weeks passed, the west wall of the dining room looked less and less like paneling and more and more like "Ode to an Alphabet."

This also made for some sparkling dinner conversation. We sit around the table in the following manner: I sit on one end, facing south; Rhonda sits on the other end, facing north; Joy and Jesse are on one side, facing east; and Jeffrey and John sit on the other side, facing the west wall.

It seemed like whenever there was a lull in the conversation, Jeffrey and John would stare straight ahead at the west wall. One look at the sounds of the alphabet in pictures and . . . well, one little boy couldn't resist. From a small voice facing the west wall would come the now familiar strains:

> "Aaa, aaa, apple, bh, bh, ball
> Ck, ck, cat, and dh, dh, doll
> Eh, eh, egg, and fff, fff, fan
> Ggh, ggh, goat, and hhh, hhh, hand."

Yes, the little guy couldn't control himself. He loved that song and the wall was so much more exciting than the dull dinner conversation. He'd just break right into the song and he'd sing it all the way through.

Mama and Dad were so proud of our little man who could belt out such a great tune. And pride filled Joy, Jesse, and especially Jeffrey.

For, you see, the little singer was *John!*

He had surprised us all by picking right up on the sounds of the letters. Here he was, not even four years old, and he was a vocabulary vocalist.

See, that little guy had been consistently sneaking out to the dining room each afternoon, when he was supposed to be in taking a nap. He had eavesdropped so diligently that he was as proficient in the skills as his older brother and sister.

"Well, chalk up another advantage for Union Station Education," announced Rhonda. "Instead of each child being totally separated in individual grade levels, we have a sort of one-room schoolhouse where the younger ones can benefit from the instruction we give the older ones!"

I was about to agree, when John once again interrupted the silence.

"Aaa, aaa, apple, bh, bh, ball."

"You're right, babe!" I yelled over the soloist. "We're gonna have some readers on our hands real soon."

"You bet!" echoed Jeffrey.

And before too long, it was true.

After he had learned all his letters, Jeffrey learned blending and phonics and all that good stuff that transforms a child from illiterate to literate.

Mama faithfully plugged away at the whole process, and it paid off.

Each evening I would use dinner time as an occasion to review what had taken place that particular day. As long as I live, I'll never forget the night Jeffrey met me at the door with a book in his hand.

"Sit down, Dad, and listen!"

I welcomed a five-year-old wonder up onto my lap, and he proceeded to read me a story. It was a simple story about a bat and a cat and a boy and a toy. I don't even remember the plot, but it's one of the few books in my life that brought tears to my eyes.

My wife had taught my little boy to read. All by herself. All by himself. I still can't get over it. Maybe it's no big deal to someone else, but to me it was a demonstration of Union Station Education at its best.

So I tip my hat to my wonderful wife.

And I encourage my kids to bring an aaa, aaa, apple for their terrific teacher.

7

Union Station Celebration

Each one of the four seasons provides its own special contribution to Union Station Education. But I don't need to think twice about my personal favorite: I'm a real fan of the fall.

From the time I was a boy growing up in the Philadelphia area, I can remember anxiously anticipating the end of summer heat and the beginning of nature's greatest show: the autumn leaves. There's an incredible mix in the coloring of the fall foliage that is both majestic and simple.

These are the months where you move from the patio, indoors to a cozy spot by the fireplace. Our crew has had plenty of great times in both locations and to me, that's part of family life at its best.

As Rhonda and I sat in bed one night, reflecting over the day, she shared similar feelings. "I'm real excited about September, October, November, and December this year," she sighed. "I think we can make some valuable contributions to the total education of the kids during those months."

"Yeah, look at all the extra educational television available in September," I volunteered. "We can see major league baseball *and* NFL football during that month—it's terrific."

Rhonda ignored my statement just as I had ignored hers. "I'm thinking of the holidays that we celebrate during those months," she continued. "I want to pass on some family traditions to the kids about Thanksgiving and Christmas—even Halloween if we can."

She was gaining my attention. Family traditions are important to both of us, so I started to focus in on her words. She went on.

"Did you know that the University of Nebraska did research on what makes a family strong?"

I shook my head.

"They researched three thousand families in order to see what made strong families tick. I was just reading some of the findings the other day and the whole area of family traditions surfaced."

She pulled the book *Secrets of Strong Families* by Nick Stinnett off the nightstand. "Listen to this!" she exclaimed.

Traditions in families have been described as the "we always" of family life: We always have cider at Halloween; We always have hugs at bedtime; We always . . . Strong families often told us about their family traditions. . . . Holidays are special times. We enjoy decorating the house, fixing special foods. We have traditions for most holidays—jack-o'-lanterns at Halloween, a food basket to give to a needy family at Thanksgiving, a trip to the cemetery on Memorial Day. . . .

One of the most apparent demonstrations of the spiritual nature is participation in religious traditions and rituals. Tradition and ritual have been criticized at times as being mechanical and meaningless—empty motion. Certainly that can be the case. But for our strong families, tradition and ritual are outward expressions of a deeper commitment.

She paused again, closed the book, and looked up at me.

"I love it when people can say, 'We always did such and such as a part of our Thanksgiving,' or, 'We never missed doing blank on Christmas Eve.' I think those traditions bring a certain sense of security to those who participate in them. That's what I want for our family, don't you, Bill?"

"I sure do," I responded. "If *total education* means positive family memories, then count me in."

The next morning at breakfast the topic of conversation was the holiday nearest at hand—Halloween. "What's something about Halloween here at our house that's special to you guys?" Rhonda asked.

All four responded in unison, "CANDY!"

"Okay," replied Rhonda. "That's the easy answer. Now what else makes Halloween special around here?"

This time there was a longer period of silence. It was Jesse who volunteered the first answer.

"Well, I like it that we always get a punkin and that Daddy helps us carve it into a funny face."

"A jack-o'-lantern," Rhonda said aloud as she wrote it down in her notebook. "That's a very good idea, Jesse. Every year we'll be sure to have a jack-o'-lantern."

"And when I get bigger," interrupted John, "I'll be able to use the knife to make my own kind of face on the punkin!"

"You're right, Johnny," I smiled. "And that day will be here before you know it!" I looked over at Rhonda and we knew those words were all too true.

"I know what I like about Halloween at our house," came the voice of Joy. "I like that most of the other kids go out and buy costumes at the store, but we always make our own from stuff we have around the house."

Rhonda began writing again. She looked up and said, "I'm glad you feel that way, Joy. It's a little more work to do it that way, but that's why we do it, so it will be a special memory for all of you."

So, armed with two clear evidences for family tradition, we could at least say we always have a jack-o'-lantern at Halloween and we always make our own costumes.

My favorite recollection of homemade costumes is the year we were big on pancake makeup and spray paint for the hair. Joy and Jesse were all decked out in clown outfits sent to us straight from the sewing machine of Rhonda's mother. We painted their faces white and added the appropriate red lips, red cheeks, and black eye makeup. We spray painted their hair a fluorescent color and concluded these were clearly clowns of class.

Jeffrey put on his cowboy suit, which was made up of his western shirt, jeans, vest with the leather fringes, boots, hat, guns, holster, and a Lone Ranger mask. "If people don't give me candy, I'm gonna say, 'Stick 'em up, Mister!' " Jeffrey enjoyed talking tough.

"No need, Jeffrey," I countered. "If folks give you a hard time, you send in the clowns; they'll take care of it for you."

Without question, the greatest creative challenge of the evening was John. He decided he wanted to dress up in a more unusual manner than the others.

"I wanna be a punkin," he stated in a matter-of-fact voice. "I don't wanna be a person, I wanna be a punkin."

After a creative brainstorming session, we latched onto an idea. We borrowed a T-shirt from a friend of ours. This was no ordinary T-shirt. It was a Tampa Bay Buccaneer T-shirt. And, of course, it was in one of the team colors—orange.

We turned the T-shirt inside out so the Buc's emblem was no longer visible. We put the shirt on John and began stuffing him with every pillow in the house. I used one of my old belts to strap in the bottom of the shirt. That way, we wouldn't lose any tonnage.

I backed up to admire our work. I was pleased. Rhonda wasn't. "We've got to do something about his head. He looks like a pumpkin with a head on top."

"That's what it is," I replied.

"I'VE GOT IT!" she suddenly exclaimed. "Put more pillows in, up to his chin. I'll take care of the chin on up."

So I grunted and groaned to get a couple more pillows in. As I struggled, Rhonda returned with the answer:

Orange spray makeup.

She applied it generously to both face and hair. Before long my little boy was totally transformed into the official object of October.

"Wow!" he exclaimed. "Look at me! I'm a cool-lookin' punkin!" He started to run out to show his friends, but he turned back and yelled, "Thanks, Mama, thanks, Daddy, you guys are really 'pecial."

His blue eyes never looked happier. Maybe it was the contrast to the orange skin. But whatever the reason, Halloween was heavenly.

Union Station Celebrations became quite the happening things. As we left October and welcomed November, Thanksgiving became the topic of discussion. We had some well-established traditions already in place for Thanksgiving, so the kids grew more and more excited.

That's half the fun of it, I thought, *anticipating the holiday. I can remember counting the days till Thanksgiving.*

With that thought my mind drifted back to a family tradition we had when I was a boy. It involved my favorite day of the year—Thanksgiving.

My memories were vivid of the hardest-working man I'd ever known. I called him Dad. He was a railroad man, working on the Reading Railroad in Philadelphia during my growing-up years. The railroad life was a demanding one. The trains ran even on holidays. Even on Thanksgiving.

But my fondest childhood memory is based on the fact that every Thanksgiving the Reading Railroad would have one extra employee—me.

That was the best part of Thanksgiving for me. I *always* went to work with Dad on that special Thursday.

I'd sit at the desk next to his and watch him make early-morning calls to check out the action there at the yard. I'd run to keep up with him as we'd walk the tracks that made up the grounds of the Port Richmond Car Shop. Then we'd return to the office and I'd play with my favorite toy of his—the typewriter.

I don't know what was more exhilarating, banging out letters to imaginary folks on that old Underwood or just being a desk away from Dad. It's gotta be the latter.

Somebody might argue the fact that Thanksgiving with my father wasn't exactly the best example of "quality time." Well, if it had to be highly structured, with a time of verbal teaching, I guess it wasn't quality time in the strictest terms.

But for a little blond-haired kid, it was a time of the utmost quality.

My train ride to the past was routed back to Union Station as I heard the kids barking out the special Thanksgiving events at the Butterworths of *this* generation.

"We always eat turkey!" yelled Jeffrey.

"We always watch the Cowboys play football!" chimed in Jesse.

"We always have friends over to join us for dinner!" cheered Joy.

"We always have chili, not turkey!" interrupted John.

"No, sweetie," corrected Rhonda in her soothing way, "you have your days a little mixed up. We always have turkey on Thanksgiving and we always have chili the day after Thanksgiving. Do you remember why we do that, John?"

"Yeah, because we eat chili the day we put up the Christmas tree!" And with that comment, the kids exploded with enthusiasm.

Another Butterworth tradition had been uncovered. Thanksgiving is more than just a day for our crew. We actually make Thanksgiving a four-day celebration, from Thursday through Sunday. It's both a time of thanks and a time of preparation for the next big event—Christmas.

Everybody laughs at us, but we've been doing it this way for years. The day after Thanksgiving we head out and pick up a Christmas tree from the nearby Christmas tree farm. Lots of folks are out there reserving trees to be cut down later, but all the Butterworths find the tree that's just right for our place and say, "Cut it down, please . . . we'll take it with us."

"It'll never live to see Christmas!" come the taunts of the scoffers. But we haven't lost one yet!

Another tradition is that the tree will always be a little too big to fit in the door. This brings about Daddy's annual battle with the branches. It's a gory sight, folks, but ultimately man overcomes tree. Sweaty, red-faced, and bruised, Daddy sets the tree in the stand and ties the tree to any piece of furniture that will help it live through the love of four kids.

"We always play the first Christmas songs of the season when we decorate the tree!" Joy reminds us as she uncovers records, both old and new, with our favorite carols.

Christmas records always have the children's seal of approval—lots of scratches on the records, indicating years of use. We have good variety in our musical tastes: portions of the *Messiah,* portions of the *Nutcracker,* portions of "Jingle Bell Rock."

Decorating the tree is another special occasion. Rhonda and I help the kids with each ornament to be hung. There are no garden-variety generic tinsel and balls for the Butterworth tree. No, each ornament has a story.

"Jesse," Rhonda calls, "here's a little angel you made in Sunday school when you were two years old."

"Wow," responds Jesse, obviously impressed with his work.

"Here's an ornament made for Joy when it was just the three of us," I explain as I hand Joy a little ball with her name on it.

"This little star has a picture of a baby in the middle. Who is that little cutie?" Everyone looks carefully, because there's a star for each child.

"That's me, Mama!" screams Jeffrey with a sense of pride. "Was I really a cutie?" With that, Rhonda sweeps up a little guy who's still a cutie and gives him a great big hug.

As you can imagine, this makes decorating the tree quite a time-consuming extravaganza. But what's the big rush, anyway? Tree-trimming is only once a year. Why hurry through it?

I think the Christmas season is good for my patience. When I come to the end of my rope in hanging ornaments or stringing lights or wrapping gifts, I just need to turn around and observe the eyes of my children. Eyes like saucers, big and round. Eyes full of wonder, enjoyment, and innocence. Eyes that say through their look, "Dad, slow down, it's okay."

Yes, those kids of mine seem ecstatic just to stand next to me at the tree and hang ornaments. It's an ecstasy I once felt while typing imaginary letters at the desk next to Dad's.

Finally the big moment arrives. Daddy climbs on a stool and puts the silver star on top of the tree. We didn't have a star when we first celebrated as a family. So instead of buying one, we made one from cardboard and tinfoil. It's not very impressive, yet it's perfect. It is the crown for a tree that is uniquely Union Station in appearance.

And that's what makes it so grand.

The reward for this day of Union Station Celebration is Mama's homemade chili. One of the reasons it's so good is that Rhonda makes it early and cooks it all day. Think about that statement. All day the aroma of homemade happiness floats through the house. No one is unaffected by it. By the time the tree is decorated, the chili is top priority on everyone's list.

By the way, there is one tradition my wife holds to that I am unable to support. As she ladles the steaming chili into crocks, she tells the kids, "Don't forget the jar of peanut butter!"

That's right, folks. The kids run to the pantry and shout,

"We always mix peanut butter into our chili!" And they always do.

I don't. That is distinctively Rhonda. She ate peanut butter with everything as a child growing up, and apparently she is unable to shake off this vice as an adult.

Anyway, we all gather by the tree and eat our glorious victory feast. Rhonda and I look at the peaceful looks on the faces of the children and we look at each other with an expression of thanks.

Later that evening, the kids are nestled all snug in their beds, and Rhonda and I sit by the tree feeling half dead.

"Thanks, sweetie," Rhonda says as she squeezes my hand. "I know it takes a lot of work to do Thanksgiving the way we do it and then immediately follow it up with the Christmas tree. But it means so much to the kids. They love it, you know!"

"*They* love it? *I* love it!" I sneak in. "Thank you for all the extra effort to prepare the Thanksgiving feast and then turn around and prepare chili from scratch so that we can have this special tradition."

As we hug each other, we think our separate thoughts, yet they are alike. Part of Union Station Education is Union Station Celebration. If we can use the extra hours we have with our kids to help them see the importance we place on our family and visually demonstrate that concept by developing family traditions, we're headed for success in our adventure.

Family traditions and holiday celebrations are important. They should be part of every home's curriculum. We really come into our own when we hit December. Christmas at Union Station is wonderful.

Thinking about Christmas gets me all worked up inside. I thank God for the greatest gift in human form He's ever given me. My little home-school teacher has changed my life. As we sit there, hugging by the Christmas tree, I whisper in her ear: "I thought of another tradition. The night we put up the Christmas tree, you and I *always* come back later and smooch."

And that year was no different.

8

Christmas Curriculum

We always felt a little cramped trying to squeeze Christmas into just one day. There's too much to do, too much to say, too much to eat. So we expanded it to a more suitable time frame.

It takes a month to celebrate Christmas at our place.

Christmas at Union Station begins the last Thursday of November and goes all the way through December 25.

Even the curriculum takes a turn toward the reason for the season. Joy Lynn adds a new dimension to her reading skills by daily rehearsing her important part in our Christmas Eve party. She reads aloud the *real* Christmas story from the Bible. It's quite a challenge for her, and she faithfully practices every day during our monthlong time of remembrance.

Let's face it: The rigidity of a public-school curriculum would not allow for the flexibility we are able to provide. Of course it's easy to understand the need for the rigidity with one poor soul in charge of twenty-seven little lives. But home-education is more tutorial in basis and the advantages of that system are seen daily.

Perhaps the most fun in the Christmas curriculum is the heavy emphasis on arts and crafts. This direction came as a result of a typical conversation during the last week of November. No prompting was necessary, no questions were asked. The kids just started volunteering information that was important to them.

"I wanna new bicycle for Christmas!"

"I wanna new set of Legos and a battery-powered, remote-control, super-rad Trans Am!"

"I wanna Cabbage Patch doll and a new pair of roller skates and a Monopoly game!"

"I wanna rocking horse and a GI Joe Commando Pontoon Base Headquarters and a baseball glove and a Uno game and a skateboard and a—"

"ENOUGH, ENOUGH, PLEASE ENOUGH!" I interrupted with the force of a tornado. "Where do you think all the money comes from to buy all this stuff?"

"That's why you go to work, Dad," was the cool, calm reply of Jeffrey. "I need a new Wiffle ball bat too."

"Kids, come here and sit down." It was Rhonda sensing the tension in the air. "We need to have a talk about Christmas gifts."

Her timing was perfect. After tabulating what all those gifts would cost me, I had run out to the kitchen for a paper bag to breathe into.

"Christmas is a time for gifts," Rhonda began. She was stopped short by a loud "HOORAY!" from all the kids.

"But," she pressed on, "and this is a very important point, so listen carefully."

All ears perked up.

"Christmas is more than a time for gifts. More importantly it's a time for *giving!*"

Her big point was met with silent stares.

"You see, Christmas is all about Jesus," she continued.

"Christmas is Jesus' birthday!" announced John, as if it were news hot off the press.

"That's right, John. When we celebrate Christmas, we celebrate God's greatest gift to us. That gift is His Son, Jesus."

"And I remember when the wise men visited," Joy reflected. "They gave gifts to Baby Jesus."

"Joy, that's exactly right," commented Rhonda, realizing all those rehearsals of the Christmas story seemed to be sinking in.

"So, you see, kids," she went on, "the emphasis at Christmastime should be on *giving,* not on getting."

The pleasant thought of giving was interrupted by Mr. Bottom Line, alias Jesse.

"But, Mom, I'm broke. How can I give gifts to people if I don't even have a few bucks?"

"Well," Rhonda pondered, "I think the best kinds of gifts aren't from a store anyway. The best kinds are gifts you make with your own hands. To me, it just makes it even more special that way."

The kids slowly looked around the circle at one another. I was amazed at the nonverbal messages that were being passed around. The first looks were the "Gee, what a dumb idea" looks. But as each of them began to think of homemade gifts they could create, the expressions quickly changed to "Hey, this could be fun" looks.

When I saw that look, I knew we had 'em.

The first order of business was to consolidate the stockpile of resources we had from which the gifts were to be made. *What can I make my gift out of?* we all asked ourselves. The question was not easily answered at first. But gradually, like a snowball from the first snow of December, the possibility list got bigger and bigger as we rolled it along.

We're not talking fancy, folks. We're talking practical. Here's the kind of stuff that came together in the "Soon to be a Christmas present" pile:

- Construction paper
- White paste and tape
- Magic Markers
- Plywood scraps
- Old shoe boxes
- Paper towel tubes
- Paints and brushes
- Crayons
- Old clothes
- Hammers
- Saws
- Old bed sheets
- 70 percent of the parts of an old window fan
- Picture frames
- Yarn
- Felt
- Styrofoam cups and plates
- Years of old magazines
- Scissors
- Rocks
- Old bleach jugs
- A large roll of "newspaper"-type paper
- Old, too tiny to use, pencil stubs
- Frozen orange juice cans (empty, please).

And that was just the two dozen items we gathered first!

"Now," said Rhonda, "you can make whatever you want out of this great pile of materials! But before you do, we're all going to make something together."

As she said this, she began to unroll long sheets of the "newspaper"-type paper out on the family room floor.

"Everyone go wash your hands and hustle on back here!"

The kids zoomed and quickly returned with clean hands and wide eyes.

"What are we gonna make, Mama?"

"That's a lot of paper, Mama. It must be something real big."

"Is it an important present, Mama?"

"Very important," she replied, indicating she was ready to announce the project. "When you find your gifts under the tree on Christmas morning, what's the first thing you do with them?"

Joy yelled, "Unwrap 'em and play with 'em!"

"Correct!" Rhonda answered. "So, in order to *un*wrap your gifts, those of us who give gifts have to . . .?"

"Wrap them!" smiled Jesse. "I've got it! We're gonna make wrapping paper!"

"You guessed it!" beamed their mama. "But not just any old wrapping paper. We're going to make *personalized* wrapping paper!"

With that, she started passing out the paint brushes and unscrewing the lids from the paint jars. "Okay, you each have your own brush and you each have a long strip of paper. Do whatever you want to personally decorate this wrapping paper. You can paint pictures or make designs or—"

"Fingerpaint!" announced Jeffrey. He already was participating in his own suggestion.

I was amazed at the creativity I was watching in our home. Each child was totally absorbed in his or her own creation. I was pleased to see there wasn't a lot of "copying" from someone else's paper.

Joy was painting beautiful little rainbows and hearts in a feminine, petite design. She smiled as she painted.

Jesse was developing a rather elaborate seascape. There were sailboats and waves and clouds and docks. As he painted, his tongue would find its way out of his mouth and would eventually rest on his upper lip.

Jeffrey was fingerpainting furiously. He was a "free form" artist, showing great creativity in his description-defying designs. He had a determined look on his face, obviously in deep concentration.

John was placing his entire hand in the paint and making handprints of different colors in a random pattern on the paper. His look stated clearly, "I'm doing all this by myself, with no help from nobody!"

As the children reached the end of their rolls of paper, they cleaned up their brushes, went back to the bathroom, washed up, and returned to contemplate the gifts they could make.

Jesse started right in on his favorite stuff: wood scraps. He whispered to me, "I'm gonna make a stool for Mama to use in the kitchen. You know, to reach the stuff way up high?"

I nodded and we both giggled as we snuck his necessary items out into the garage where he could work in secret.

Joy carried the old magazines, white paste, construction paper, and scissors into her room. "I'm gonna cut out pictures of sports guys and put them together in a big picture for Jesse," she whispered to Rhonda.

"Oh, you mean a collage," Rhonda whispered back.

"College or pro, anything to do with sports," Joy answered as she scurried off to work.

"Mama," whispered Jeffrey. "I'm gonna take these old clothes and make some play costumes for John."

Rhonda nodded in approval as he ran off to his room.

That left little John staring at the pile. He was obviously uninspired. "Everybody's got an idea 'cept me," he said as his eyes began to tear up. "It's not fair. I don't know what to do."

"Why don't we take this old frozen-orange-juice can and make it into a pencil holder for Jeffrey?" Rhonda suggested. That's all the motivation John needed. His eyes, still wet, smiled brightly.

"Yeah, Mama, that's it!" he beamed. "I can take these old little pencils and tape them around the can so Jeffrey knows what's 'posed to go in it!"

"Great idea, John!" Rhonda replied. "We can put a piece of felt around it first, then put the little pencils on the felt. Okay?"

"You bet!" came the reply from a happy craftsman.

December was a glorious month. The Christmas curriculum was a real boost to everyone's excitement. Whenever Rhonda's pregnancy put her in bed, the kids would go off to their "hideouts" and work on their gifts. And when she was up and around, they would make things together.

I'd come home during my lunch hour and see any variety of newly created objects. At one point, Rhonda and the kids all sat around the dining room table and made Christmas tree ornaments for friends and neighbors: little styrofoam-cup angels and tiny Christmas trees made from green felt. Add a loop of red yarn and they're ready to hang from a good friend's tree.

Some evenings we'd gather up the family and walk down the street to a neighbor's house to give them the ornament made just for them. Invariably they would feel uncomfortable and stammer out, "Uh, but, well, I don't have any gift for you."

"That's okay," Jeffrey would console. "This is Christmas and we're *givin'*, not *gettin'!*"

One night, Rhonda was in bed, reading more from her new champion in life, Susan Schaeffer Macaulay. As my wife began breathing faster, I knew she had hit a section that tickled her fancy.

"Bill, I've got to read you this portion of *For the Children's Sake*. She's talking about values and moral issues and nurturing people to maturity. I love it! That's what we were doing tonight with the gift-giving!"

Unfortunately, I was already dozing off for the night. It

was unfortunate, not for Rhonda, but for *me!* I quickly
awoke and did my best to pay attention. Rhonda began:

> We do not preach or moralize. If children are
> growing up surrounded by those who *practice* God's
> morality, they themselves will think and express
> judgments using their own minds . . .
>
> Just because a home or school is "Christian" does
> not mean that the child is being properly helped,
> grounded, educated as a whole person. We accept
> that nothing is perfect, but we try to get our prior-
> ities right. We are ready to take time and trouble to
> see that our children aren't swept off in a roaring
> tide. But we want more than that. We pray for a
> person who is like the individual mentioned in Psalm
> 1. He has grown like an oak tree by a stream. Storms
> may roar, a branch or two may snap, but the oak
> stands firmly grounded—so much so that small crea-
> tures seek shelter therein.
>
> There is no one method to achieve such a mature
> person. There is no perfect or complete situation. We
> must pray for the individual, pray for wisdom, open
> our eyes, choose priorities. We must not only talk.
> We have to serve, give, and be willing to live with
> the children. We nurture with *life*.

I reached over and pulled her closer to me. I silently
thanked God for giving me a woman with a zeal and intensity for nurturing with life. She was teaching me much.

Well, December moved along, and it was finally Christmas Eve. The kids were all abuzz, cleaning their rooms
and helping fix up the house for the Christmas Eve party.
Actually, we called it "A Birthday Party for Jesus." It

would be complete with cake and candles. The kids looked forward to it with delicious delight.

Rhonda stood back to observe the kids at work and said, "Hmm." When she says "Hmm," it ain't good.

"What's the matter, babe?" I inquired.

"The boys need haircuts. They look shaggy and sloppy."

I checked my watch. "It's kinda late, but I guess I can run them down to the barbershop real quick."

Rhonda studied her watch. "You know, I'm ahead of schedule. I could save you some time and money if I went ahead and cut their hair."

I was stunned. I was married to this woman all these years and *never* once had she mentioned that she could cut hair. "Babe, I'm shocked! I didn't know you could cut hair."

"Well...l...l," she stammered, "actually I've never cut hair before, but, but—well, I've watched other people do it, and it looks simple enough to me."

I smiled. *What a riot!* I thought. I decided to play along . . . after all, we want to make Christmas memorable, right?

"In what sort of style are you going to cut their hair?" I asked.

"I think I'll give them a sport cut," was her immediate response.

"A sport cut?" I replied. "What in the world is a sport cut?"

"You know," she said, "short on the sides and the back, and a little on the top."

"That's called a sport cut?" I mocked.

"Don't mock me," she replied.

"Sport cut," I continued. "So if Steve Sax or Kareem Abdul-Jabbar or Joe Montana sat down in a barber chair, the barber would lean over and say, 'Sport cut, Steve?' or 'Sport cut, Kareem?' or—"

"Out you go!" she interrupted. "Boys, come in here. I'm going to give you all a haircut!"

The boys ran in, partly in obedience, but partly out of curiosity. "What kind of haircut are you gonna give us?" Jesse inquired.

"Don't ask," I advised, while on my way out. "But I'll give you a hint—ask Fernando Valenzuela."

"OUT."

"Okay, okay, I'm out of here."

I sat in the room for a *long* time. I didn't hear any cries or screams, but for some reason, she wasn't releasing any of the prisoners.

Finally, after what seemed like hours, she came out. Alone.

"Now, Bill," she began calmly, "if you say anything critical, I'll break your arms and legs."

I held up my hands, indicating that I would agree to her terms.

"All right, boys, you can come out now!"

My three sons had gone into that room hours earlier. But *who* were these three alien creatures coming out of that very same room?

Their hair was hideous. There's no other way to describe it. That's it. Hideous hair. It was all chopped up, in no order or pattern. I could only conclude that *sport cut* was code for "scissors gone amok."

The silence was broken by Rhonda's painful scream, "DON'T JUST SIT THERE, DO SOMETHING!!!"

I shook my head in ignorance. "But what?"

"TAKE THEM TO THE BARBER FOR A REAL HAIR-CUT!!" she replied, totally overcome by the emotion caused by hideous hair.

"Okay, boys," I said as I sought to console Rhonda. "Go into your rooms, put on your Dodger hats, and quietly get into the car."

Fortunately, the barber wasn't too busy. He took one look at the boys and asked if we would mind if he sat down for a minute. It was then I realized I had never seen a barber *sit*.

He gained his composure and spoke in hushed tones, "Only one thing we can do to salvage these heads . . . a BUZZ!"

I nodded in silent agreement. Nothing short of the Christmas Eve Buzz could save this situation.

I gathered up my three cue balls, paid the barber, wished him a merry Christmas, and headed home.

"My head's cold," complained John.

"Mine's freezin'," piped in Jeffrey.

"Easy, boys," I replied. "Let's have a good attitude about this now. Not everyone gets a buzz haircut on Christmas Eve, you know. It's sort of special."

I have to admit, it did take some time to get used to. (I think till about mid-March for me.) But anyway, we returned home just in time for our Birthday Party for Jesus.

We sang Christmas songs, ate Christmas cookies, and passed out some presents to the friends who had joined us for the evening.

Then we sat quietly as my little princess opened her Bible and read without flaw from the second chapter of Luke:

> Now it came about in those days that a decree went out from Caesar Augustus, that a census be taken of all the inhabited earth.
>
> This was the first census taken while Quirinius was governor of Syria.
>
> And all were proceeding to register for the census, everyone to his own city.
>
> And Joseph also went up from Galilee, from the city of Nazareth, to Judea, to the city of David, which is called Bethlehem, because he was of the

house and family of David, in order to register, along with Mary, who was engaged to him, and was with child.

And it came about that while they were there, the days were completed for her to give birth.

And she gave birth to her first-born son; and she wrapped Him in cloths, and laid Him in a manger, because there was no room for them in the inn.

And in the same region there were some shepherds staying out in the fields, and keeping watch over their flock by night.

And an angel of the Lord suddenly stood before them, and the glory of the Lord shone around them; and they were terribly frightened.

And the angel said to them, "Do not be afraid; for behold, I bring you good news of a great joy which shall be for all the people; for today in the city of David there has been born for you a Savior, who is Christ the Lord.

"And this will be a sign for you: you will find a baby wrapped in cloths, and lying in a manger."

And suddenly there appeared with the angel a multitude of the heavenly host praising God, and saying,

"Glory to God in the highest, and on earth peace among men with whom He is pleased."

And it came about when the angels had gone away from them into heaven, that the shepherds began saying to one another, "Let us go straight to Bethlehem then, and see this thing that has happened which the Lord has made known to us."

And they came in haste and found their way to Mary and Joseph, and the baby as He lay in the manger.

And when they had seen this, they made known the statement which had been told them about this Child.

And all who heard it wondered at the things which were told them by the shepherds.

But Mary treasured up all these things, pondering them in her heart.

And the shepherds went back, glorifying and praising God for all that they had heard and seen, just as had been told them.

Luke 2:1–20

Joy sighed, looked up, and smiled.

We all cheered loudly. We were all so happy.

Happy for a little girl who could make it through twenty Bible verses without a hitch.

Happy for a Christmas curriculum that brought such an indescribable joy to our family.

And happy for God's greatest gift of all . . . Jesus. He's the glue that holds together Union Station.

Happy Birthday, Jesus!

9

The Blossoming of a Beauty

As the carols of Christmas surrendered to the noise of the New Year, there was a particular facet of our Birthday Party for Jesus that I couldn't get out of my mind. It wasn't the cake and candles or the gifts or even the sport cuts turned buzz.

It was my little princess reading the Bible.

Not only reading the Bible, but how *well* she did reading the Bible.

New Year's Day always gives me occasion to stop and examine the progress we've made as a family and as individuals. It was becoming abundantly clear to me that the greatest progress achieved in Union Station Education was in the life of Joy Lynn. She was transforming before my very eyes.

Yes, transforming. She was my little flower, beginning to blossom. Not so much physically, although she was growing tall, slender, and more beautiful every day, but emotional, intellectual, social, and spiritual maturity were the transformations clearly evident in her life.

But this flower didn't blossom with ease. No, there were days in the past when this little flower was stepped on and trampled. And the result of this treatment was the same in flowers as it was in humans: bruises.

But, let's be fair and put things in their proper perspective. Not all the bruises acquired by a flower are the fault of the "bruiser." Much of that is simply part of life.

Actually, many flowers are bruised because they themselves have such a delicate makeup, especially vulnerable to bruises that might leave another form of nature untouched.

That's our Joy: delicate, vulnerable, very sensitive, shy, withdrawn, and easily threatened.

But as I looked at her that Christmas Eve, I didn't see the insecure flower in hiding, but rather a person approaching full bloom.

Stanford University had recently released the results of a six-year study of matched pairs of home-schooled children and traditionally schooled children. They found the home-schoolers to be significantly more advanced in achievement, behavior, and social preparation. The research was all well and good, but now I was *experiencing* it with my own daughter. She was gaining confidence again. Reading twenty Bible verses aloud to a group of family and friends may be no problem to another kid her age, but to Joy it was a demonstration of some renewed personal security.

I saw more of the bruises of the past being overcome in her social life one Saturday afternoon in January as we sat in the family room watching "Wide World of Sports."

Jesse was busy cleaning up his baseball glove in preparation for Little League practice, which would begin in just a few weeks. Jesse is extroverted, confident, and very sociable.

Joy, on the other hand, was quiet, a follower, and tended to avoid group settings.

"Daddy," she began, pointing to the television, "I want to do what she's doing."

She was ice-skating.

"You want to learn how to ice-skate?" I clarified.

"Yeah . . . I think I really want to do that."

"There's a rink over at the mall that gives lessons," Rhonda encouraged. "We could go over and sign you up for the basics class."

"Class?" Joy interrupted. "Not just me, but other kids?"

"Yes, that's right," Rhonda answered.

Without a moment's hesitation Joy responded, "Okay, that's great. Let's go over and sign up!"

The blossoming of a social flower.

Joy did well in skating. She was nervous and tentative at first. But as she began to get the hang of it, her nervousness waned and her confidence grew. She got to the point where she couldn't wait for her Tuesday-afternoon lessons.

She started inviting her girl friends to come watch her skate. Rhonda and I had such fun watching her keep one eye on the teacher and the other on the stands to be certain family and friends watched the flower show.

But Union Station Education is a complex item. As Joy continued her education on ice, Jesse began education on first base, Jeffrey continued education with aaa, aaa, apple, and Rhonda remained constant with morning sickness—morning, noon, and night.

Tutoring would be easier if there were just one child. You could give all your attention all the time to your one student. But Joy, Jesse, and Jeffrey were all in different grades, learning different things, so Rhonda had to keep juggling.

"This afternoon we're going to do something special," Rhonda announced to Joy and Jesse one January day. "I'm going to work with Jeffrey on his letters, and while I'm doing that, you two are going to work on a very important project!"

Their eyes widened as they looked at each other, giggled excitedly, and then looked back at Mama for the directions.

"When I was a little girl, I remember a very special story. It was a story about a lighthouse. It was pages and pages about this little lighthouse. The reason the story was so special is because I *wrote* it all by myself."

The kids looked at each other again, but this time they stared at each other and slowly swallowed.

"So," Mama went on, "I want the two of you to share in the same sort of special memory. I want you to get your notebooks and pencils, go back to your rooms, and write me a story. Then tonight at dinner, we'll read the stories out loud for Daddy."

"I'm gonna write about a jet flyer," Jesse announced as he headed off to his room. That was typical Jesse—creative and quick.

Joy just walked off slowly, silently. *I wonder what's going on in her head right now,* Rhonda thought. *Creative thoughts? Or maybe another visit from that monster, insecurity?*

"You can do it, sweetie!" Rhonda encouraged Joy as she walked quietly to her room.

Well, the afternoon came and went. We were all seated at the dinner table, waiting to hear about everyone's day. Jeffrey was first with the latest report from the land of phonics. John was second with a gory tale of skateboards, sidewalks, and feet without shoes or socks. John is definitely in the "know what?" stage:

"Dad, know what?" he began. "I was outside today riding Jesse's skateboard. And ya know what? I was riding it down the sidewalk over by Jenny's house. And ya know what? I didn't see that there was a dumb old bike in the way. And ya know what? I put down my foot to stop me. And ya know what? I forgot to wear shoes and socks, so when I stopped the skateboard I hurt my toes real bad. Know what? I can show you right now."

He started to put a bloody foot on the table, when Rhonda interrupted. "John, that won't be necessary."

"Dad, ya know what? I used two whole Band-Aids on my boo-boos, but they wouldn't stick, so they're not on there anymore."

"He doesn't mean two Band-Aids, dear," clarified Rhonda. "He means two *boxes* of Band-Aids."

"Wow," I commented, "it sounds like you had quite a day." John nodded and returned to the battle with his beef.

I turned my attention to the other side of the table. Joy and Jesse had been hiding something and giggling all during John's skateboard-sidewalk story. "So, what's going on over here?" I smiled. "What did you two do today?"

In unison they responded, "We wrote our own stories and we want to read them to you!"

"Wonderful!"

"I'll go first," volunteered Jesse. I was about to remind him of the gentleman's rule of ladies first, when I saw Rhonda signal me that Jesse going first was a good idea.

He cleared his throat and began to read from his notebook:

Once upon a time there was a jet flyer and his nickname was Jake. He has the fastest jet in America. Jake got picked out of eighty-nine people and he was the best of all the men. This is what the sergeant said, "Congratulations, out of all these men you have been voted Best Jet Pilot."

A year later the war started. It was terrible. First Jake went out in a motorboat. The bad team shot a hole in the boat and Jake had a life jacket and he swam to shore. Then he changed, got into his jet, and took off. Almost every bad ship in sight was a goner.

He finally got to and blew up half of the bad team's base and of course there were still more gunmen. Jake was going slow and he was shot down and was never seen except in heaven. He was lucky. He was a Christian.

The End.

I instinctively started to applaud, and my mind was racing. "That's a great story, Jesse! You're unbelievably creative! Did you make up that story all by yourself?"

"Yup!" he beamed.

"Well, congratulations. Isn't that excellent, Mama?"

Rhonda nodded. As I was welling up with pride over my son, the writer, I caught a glance of Joy out of the corner of my eye. She had dropped her head and was nervously fidgeting with her food.

I thought, *Nice job, stupid Daddy! Nothing like going on and on over one child and putting ten tons of tension in the life of your daugher! You're in hot water now, Butterworth!*

I wanted to leave the table. I was so wrong to have put Joy under that pressure. I realized how often I had unknowingly created sibling rivalry. It was wrong, and *I* was wrong for doing it. I panicked. I reached out, squeezed

Joy's hand, and said, "You don't have to read your story
if you don't want to, Princess. We can look at it later."

"No sir, Mr. Butterworth," came the strong words of
Mrs. Butterworth. "She has a superb story and she wants
to read it to you *right now*. Isn't that correct, Joy?"

Joy looked up, blushing, and said, "Yes, Daddy, I'd like
to read you my story now."

"Well . . . great . . . terrific . . . let's hear it . . . super." I
was fumbling around like a fish in a boat. Rhonda was
giving me her "Give your child more credit" look, and I
realized she caught me in the act of discrediting. *Joy's
every bit as creative as Jesse,* I reminded myself. *She just
expresses it in different ways.*

But as my princess began her story, I realized they
expressed one thing the same way—they were both *great*
writers.

Joy read aloud from her notebook:

> Once upon a time there were crayons. Red and
> Blue were boyfriend and girlfriend. Yellow and
> Green were boyfriend and girlfriend.
>
> They were all getting married today. Then a few
> days later somebody was coming. She opened the
> crayon box, reached in for Red, Green, Yellow, and
> Blue. Red and Green knew that if she colored with
> them, that would make them sick. And when cray-
> ons get sick, they get sick!
>
> Yellow and Blue got mad and they jumped out and
> saved Red and Green. They were so happy. Now they
> wouldn't get sick.
>
> Now it was time to go on their honeymoon. They
> decided to go to another crayon box.

At this point Joy turned the page. *What do you know?*
I thought. *A two-pager!* Joy continued:

At the new crayon box they saw different colors. Then they heard footsteps and they were scared. They hid. "Ohhh, what a relief," they said. "That was a close call!" Then they realized that Pink was gone. So they opened the lid, jumped out, and saved her.

Pink did not know how to thank them. So she took them out to eat. They were all happy so they said thank you.

And so it was dinner time. Pink fixed it. They had steak, corn, fruit salad, and a pear and an orange, and lots of stuff. And they had pie. Mmmmm.

They had a fun honeymoon so far. But that was only the second day and they were going to stay there for one week. Red, Blue, Yellow, and Green were tired so they went to bed.

I winked at Rhonda as Joy turned to page 3!

And it was next morning and they were awake. Pink had breakfast waiting.

And they said, "You don't have to do all this stuff," but she said, "You guys saved me."

"We saved you, but you don't have to do all this stuff."

Pink thinks and thinks and thinks and says, "No, I want to do this."

Blue and Green were getting mad. But Pink went on to make cookies for them. And then they heard footsteps and they were all scared.

John and Jeffrey's eyes widened. They were into this suspense in total. Joy continued:

They all hid. And she went past. "Close call," they said. They had been there for a week, so now they were going to another box. It was sad for them to leave. "Come back again," they said.

And they came to another box and this one was so great. Red, Blue, Yellow, and Green went to their room to unpack. Pink had put a letter in their suitcase. It said, "Here are cookies and Hi C."

"Oh, that girl," they said. And so it was night, so they went to bed.

Next morning they had eggs, toast, and bacon. A few hours later it was lunch time.

The girl's a chip off her father's block, I thought. *She shows the time of day by naming the meal.* I smiled some more.

At this point, page 5 appeared. Yet no one moved a muscle.

They saw a big finger. It was getting a crayon out. This time it didn't get Pink. It got White out instead. So White had to get sick. Poor White. She had to die.

So everyone was crying. We never saw White again. "Bye, White," they all said.

Rhonda dabbed her eyes with her napkin. Joy continued her magnetic marvel of a story.

They were sad for a time. They were thinking and thinking what could they do to feel better, because they wanted to feel better.

She stopped to turn to page 6. She had a little trouble turning the page. As she struggled, Jesse blurted out: "Hurry up, Joy! What do the crayons do so that they'll feel better?"

"Yeah, hurry!" prodded Jeffrey and John.

Joy continued:

> "Why don't we go out to eat?" So they did.
> But it didn't help. So they tried to go swimming
> but that didn't help so they said, "Nothing will work."
> So the week was over and they were all crying when
> they left.
> When they got home to their box they told what
> happened and it was scary because a lot of the cray-
> ons were missing. "Where did they go?"
> Red said, "A very big one took them. There were
> only five left and there were sixty-four in this box.
> Only five left!"

She turned to page 7, which appeared to be the last
page. *How can she end on such a sad note?* I mused.
Anyway, she concluded:

> "We're just joking that there are only five left,"
> said Red. And the sixty-four came out. And they
> were all very happy. The end.

Our entire family sat there in a moment of stunned
silence. Our little shy, retiring flower had exploded into
bloom with a bang!

"HOORAY FOR JOY AND HER STORY!!" came the
cheerleading of her brother Jesse. No sibling rivalry at
this point. More like sibling sensitivity.

"HOORAY FOR JOY!! HOORAY FOR HER STORY!!"
The place exploded into a party. Joy got lots of hugs,
kisses, and squeezes. She had come so far. She was something else.

Her story overpowered me for several days. I was
grateful for God's hand on the life of my only daughter.
Grateful for His consistency even when I'm inconsistent

as a parent. I saw how I could more easily joke with the extroverted boys and how much I missed out on by not knowing Joy better. There's too much there to let pass by. I resolved to be more a part of the blossoming of this beauty.

It kind of all came together at the ice-skating lessons a few weeks later. As I sat in the stands and watched Joy skate, my eye was distracted by a woman holding a little baby girl, probably around two months old.

As I looked from Joy to the baby and back to Joy, I saw how Joy has enriched my life beyond measure since her arrival on August 16, 1976.

Such a helper at home. Such a willing worker. Becoming more and more a people person.

And for just a brief moment, the ice rink was a chapel and the stands were the pews. I silently prayed to God:

Dear Lord, thank You for Joy. Thank You for helping her in her life. Lord, she's so special, so sensitive. Protect her from the hurts she must experience, help her to learn to cope, to flex, and to grow. We've seen You at work in her life, Lord. I'm so very grateful. Amen.

I looked up to see my little princess on the ice. And I fought to hold back the tears of pride and joy. I guess I'm just a sucker for flowers.

10

The Tale
of the
Whale

Several months had passed since the early days of Union Station Education. Throughout those months, David Stewart made good on his promise as well. He faithfully kept tabs on how we were doing in our endeavors, and as he had promised, he made available the curriculum, teachers, and facilities of the private school where he was principal.

David's excitement had reached such a high level that he convinced the school board to begin an Independent Study Program to be of further help to home-schoolers. The program included access to the school's curriculum, grade-level and achievement testing, upkeep of the child's cumulative record, and, best of all, two teachers who served as "consultants" to the home-school families. They would plan field trips, special events, and meetings where the home-schoolers could all get together. They'd also visit us in our homes monthly to offer help and direction.

Yes, field trips, special events, and meetings all sounded great. That is, of course, unless you are pregnant. Every time an event was planned, Rhonda was too sick to participate.

As event after event went by without Union Station participation, I began to feel frustrated about our use—or non-use—of the program. One evening as Rhonda and I were cleaning up after dinner, I accidentally let my frustration show.

"I see the Independent Study Program went to the Children's Museum today," I began, looking over my shoulder at the kitchen calendar. "It says right up there on the calendar that trip was today. I don't suppose you guys made it, did you?"

"What sort of crack is that?" snapped my sweetie, as if she had been waiting for me to bring it up. "No, we didn't make it to the museum today, as you well know. I was lucky to get out of bed today. The baby was twisting and turning and I couldn't get comfortable, and John was overtired and whiny all day, and Jeffrey and Jesse got into a big fight, and Joy—"

"Okay, okay," I interrupted. "You didn't get to go on the field trip today." We turned away from each other and continued our cleanup in uncomfortable silence.

"It just seems like a waste of money," I mumbled in barely audible tones.

"What? What was that?" Rhonda barked. "Did I hear you mention money?"

Money is like dessert at our house—a special treat, but never enough of it.

"Answer me, Bill. Did you say something about money?"

116

I weakly admitted my error. "I was just sorta thinking out loud that we're paying to be in this Independent Study Program and that's fine, as long as we use it. We just don't seem to use it. That's all."

"That's all?"

"Yes."

"Well, did it ever occur to you that I'm doing the best I can?" Her voice trembled from anger and frustration. "Did it ever occur to you that there are *two* parents in this household? Did it ever occur to you that I don't ever see *you* involved in the Independent Study Program either?"

I waited in silence a few seconds in order to see if there would be any more "Did it ever occur to you" statements in addition to those already given. When it appeared she was finished, I spoke.

"I *do* appreciate all the work you're doing, babe. I *know* you're doing the very best you can. I guess I didn't realize how much of this whole thing I was resting on your shoulders. I guess I've kind of shirked some of my responsibility, huh?"

"Not just your responsibility, your privilege. *Everything* I read about home-schooling, *everything* I hear about home-schooling, *all of it* constantly reminds me of the advantage to the child, the mother, *and* the father. Dr. Moore speaks of it, Susan Schaeffer Macaulay speaks of it, Dr. Dobson speaks of it, John Holt—"

"Okay, okay, you've made your point," I protested.

"Bill, we have our kids at home so *we* can be a vital part of their educational experience. Do *you* feel like a vital part?"

I hung my head. "No, not really."

"Well, sweetie, the kids need you," she continued in deep sincerity. "They want a daddy who knows them, loves them, plays with them, and helps teach them."

I started to develop a tiny lump in my throat.

"And, Bill," she paused, "*I* really need you too." With that, she reached over and we hugged. I clumsily knocked over the jug of drinking water left out on the counter and it rolled into the sink. So there we stood, a man and a pregnant woman, trying to hug in the midst of drinking water, dishwater, and tears. Little did I realize that this wet moment would lead to even more water.

"Babe, I really do want to be a bigger part in the kids' schooling," I said as I was toweling off. "So what do you think I could do?"

Rhonda walked over to the calendar and studied the January page very carefully. Her expression changed and she said, "Well, look at this; this is just perfect!"

She was pointing to two words written in by Tuesday, January 29.

"*Whale Watch?* What in the world is a Whale Watch?"

Rhonda beamed from ear to ear. "Sweets, a Whale Watch is just what the doctor ordered to get you involved with Union Station Education!"

I was feeling both pleased and uneasy at the same time. "Okay, so it's a great chance for me to get involved, but that still doesn't answer my question. What is it?"

"Well, it's just what it says it is," explained Rhonda. "You go out on a boat and watch the whales!"

"Watch the whales do what?"

"Swim, I guess."

"We go out on boats and watch whales swim?" I parroted back her definition with lots of sarcasm.

"Bill, it's educational!"

I shook my head in disbelief, but she continued.

"Look, it'll be fun. All the people in the Independent Study Program have chartered a boat to go out and see the whales. There is a short program this Friday night up at the school that explains what will happen. Why don't we go up there and check it out?"

I agreed. Reluctantly. But I agreed.

Rhonda had me over a barrel. Having been married to her for all these years, I knew there was no way she'd go out on a boat. Just looking at a boat made her seasick. Even when she wasn't pregnant. Add pregnancy to this equation and you have all fingers pointing to Dad as the man they'd soon call Father Field Trip.

Friday night arrived and, much to our surprise, Rhonda felt well enough to go with us. The four kids piled into the car, followed by Mom and Dad. After driving four blocks down our street, we remembered that the evening was beginning with a potluck dinner. Our pot was still in luck back in our refrigerator. As I turned the car around to return home, Joy delivered the commentary descriptive of our life:

"We're never on time anywhere, because we always forget something and hafta go back home to get it!"

I winced. She was right. It hurts to be late, especially at potlucks. The early bird gets the best food. The rest of us get the worms.

When we finally arrived at the school, we hustled on into the cafeteria. David Stewart had saved us a table, so we were able to sit right down. I grabbed four plates and dished up potluck for the kids. Rhonda dished up potluck for herself and her hubby.

The lights started blinking on and off, which was the signal that the program was about to begin. Rhonda and I looked at our almost untouched plates of food and turned to look at each other. I could see in Rhonda's eyes the look that said, "When you come late to a potluck, you not only eat what's left, you eat quickly or not at all."

I just sat there and blinked in agreement as everyone else cleared their plates and turned their chairs around to see the podium and the screen.

Mrs. McIntire, one of the two teachers overseeing the

Independent Study Program, called the meeting to order. "Moms and Dads, boys and girls, we're in for a special treat tonight. As you all know, next week we'll be going on a field trip to the Pacific Ocean."

All the kids cheered.

"We're going on a Whale Watch! So, in order to be prepared for the Whale Watch, we've invited our expert on whales to tell us all about them. Please welcome Mrs. Harris."

Everyone politely clapped as Mrs. Harris stepped to the podium and began doing her thing. "Next Tuesday, all of you will have such a unique occasion out on the water."

The kids were all wide-eyed.

"You'll get to see up close the gray whale. The whales will be swimming south from the Arctic. They come down south here because the Arctic water is cold in the winter. They're on their way to Baja, California." She shivered for effect, and I noticed several in the audience did the same.

"But when spring is near, they'll be heading home."

Lots of the kids smiled at that point, including our four. *Isn't it great to see kids smile,* I thought, *when someone talks about going home?*

"How many of you think the gray whale has big teeth?" Almost all the kids quickly raised their hands to indicate their vote. "Well, guess what? The gray whale doesn't have big teeth!"

The kids looked surprised.

"As a matter of fact, the gray whale doesn't have any teeth!" The shock of the moment was broken by a little girl who appeared to be about seven years old.

"Gray whales are just like my grandma!" she stated in a matter-of-fact tone. "No teeth."

Mrs. Harris continued, "Instead of teeth, the gray whale

has something called *baleen*. Bay rhymes with gray, leen rhymes with seen. *Baleen*. Say it with me."

We all repeated in unison, "Baleen."

"Baleen grows from the whale's upper jaw. It feels like your fingernails."

Everyone immediately grabbed their fingernails to get the idea.

"Whales eat plankton, which is drifting or floating animal or plant life. The baleen serves as a filter. It keeps the food in, but lets out the big stuff that they don't want to eat. It's like a big brush!"

At this point she had some great photos to put on the screen. Something else of interest was starting to occur: Mrs. Harris had caught the attention of the children from the beginning. But now she was luring in the adults as well. She was doing a masterful job.

"Boys and girls, did you know that a whale is a mammal?" Most of the kids shook their heads. "Remember this: Mammals are warm-blooded, have hair, have live births, and nurse their young. Can you repeat those four phrases with me?"

"Warm-blooded, have hair, have live births, and nurse their young," came the response of children *and* adults.

She clicked her little clicker and a slide appeared of a whale's top. "This is the blowhole," continued Mrs. Harris. "They are nostrils on top of the whale to blow out air. When they blow out the air, it mixes with ocean water and it looks like a mist coming out. This is how we will be able to find the whales next Tuesday."

I leaned forward in my seat, excited over the prospect of finding a gray whale.

"During migration, gray whales surface every one to six minutes in order to breathe. Between their breathing and footprints, we'll find 'em!"

"FOOTPRINTS?" came the cry of the crowd. "Whales

don't have feet, do they?" We were all a little unsure by now. After all, we all thought they had teeth.

"No," laughed Mrs. Harris. "They don't have feet, but they have a tail called a fluke. They kick their flukes and it leaves marks in the ocean, just like your feet leave footprints in the sand."

She clicked to a close-up of a fluke. The fluke was horizontal, not vertical, so it could leave a very noticeable imprint in the water.

"Well, boys and girls,"—she paused—"and Moms and Dads, I have two more slides to show you. If we're real fortunate next Tuesday, we may see a gray whale do one of these maneuvers." She clicked to the next slide, showing a whale lifting his head out of the water.

"Wow!" gasped all the kids, young *and* old.

"This is called 'spyhopping,' " said Mrs. Harris. "No one really knows why the gray whales do this. But every now and then, they'll stick their head up like they're taking a bow."

We all smiled, excitedly. Everyone had the same look on their face. It was a look that said, "Will *we* see some spyhopping on Tuesday?"

Mrs. Harris pushed on. "Now, if we're *very* fortunate, we will see a gray whale breach!" And with that she put on the final slide.

Everyone gasped. It was a shot of a gray whale leaping almost clear out of the water.

"No one knows why whales breach, either," remarked Mrs. Harris. "But they leap in the air and fall backwards with a huge splash!"

We were all mesmerized.

"Well, that concludes my presentation. I'll turn the program back over to Mrs. McIntire. Thank you for your attention."

And with that, Mrs. Harris received a standing ovation!

Driving home that evening, the kids were climbing the walls of the car.

"I wanna see the footprints first!"

"I wanna see a breach!"

"I'll settle for a spyhopper!"

"I wanna watch their blowhole work!"

Rhonda and I looked at each other and I said, "Well, I guess I owe you an apology. I made fun of the whole idea of a Whale Watch when you first brought up the idea. But I'll have to admit, I'm really excited about it now."

"I accept your apology," Rhonda responded. Then she added, "It looks like so much fun, I could be almost persuaded to come along."

My eyes lit up.

"But I said *almost*," she whispered sweetly in my ear.

Tuesday finally arrived, and Joy, Jesse, and Jeffrey piled into the car with me. John was still a little young and just the tiniest bit afraid, so he volunteered to stay home and keep Mama company.

We pulled up to the parking lot of the school and jumped into a big yellow school bus. I guess this was pretty normal stuff for the kids, but, boy, did I ever flash back. For a brief moment, I was back in fourth grade, riding Mr. Mason's Bus Six to William Davis Elementary School. It was a good time in my childhood, yet even in fourth grade the pressure of peers was already setting in. I wasn't just a fourth grader. I was a fat fourth grader. And kids can be merciless on a blond blimp.

I came back to reality only to discover something that wasn't part of my background:

Our yellow bus was tooling down a freeway.

"Well, so much for quaint little streets and bus stops on the corner," I sighed. This was L.A. life in the fast lane.

We pulled up at the dock and the Independent Study Program piled out. The moms and dads gathered their kids together and we anxiously boarded our ship.

Our boat launched and slowly, steadily, sailed out into the blue Pacific. It was chilly. After all, it was January at sea.

We'd been out just long enough for the little ones to get antsy, when all of a sudden a bullhorn went off at full blast.

"Boys and girls, this is your captain," came the voice over the loudspeaker. "We've sighted some grays two miles out on the port side."

"*Port* . . . that's left," a helpful father reminded us. He seemed more comfortable in these surroundings. I guessed some navy in his background.

At the announcement of whales on the port, the entire list of passengers moved to the port side of the ship. Apparently the boat could take it, but I still felt I should ask for volunteers to stand on the right—er—starboard.

Two miles later, we found the captain to be correct. The excitement level on that little boat was absolutely contagious. Soon the stars of the show came on stage.

"Look, everybody, footprints!" I beamed with pride as I heard the sighting coming from Jesse. Soon all of us began to see the footprints left by the whale's fluke.

"A BLOWHOLE!!" came another excited voice. As if we were all on cue, we'd point in unison and exclaim, "WOW!"

It was amazing to me how the children's attention span was expanded for an activity like this one. Flukes and blowholes occupied the better part of the morning.

"Well, folks," bellowed the captain via the loudspeaker, "it's time to turn around and head back to dock."

A wet blanket hit the Whale Watch.

"No, no, no," the kids screamed. "We can't go yet! We haven't seen a spyhop or a breach!"

But the captain wasn't listening. The little vessel was already beginning its turn.

It just didn't seem fair. The kids hung their heads; some were even crying. To be totally factual, a lot of adults were experiencing similar disappointment.

As the boat chugged back to the pier, most parents found themselves in the position of chief consoler. Bits and pieces could be heard around the deck.

"But we saw lots of footprints, son!"

"Don't cry. We'll come back out another time."

"Think about all the flukes we saw!"

The consoling was interrupted by the newest villain on the ship—the captain—once again on the loud-speaker.

"Folks, if you'll look off the port side again, you'll see some grays unusually close to shore!"

With that word, we all turned to port just in time to have our breath taken away.

There, in all its beauty and majesty, was the most in-credible sight of the day—a perfect breach! That big old gray whale leaped out of the water almost completely and fell back into the ocean with a giant splash.

It was lovely, but also quick. If the captain hadn't made the announcement when he did, most of us would have missed it. It was the perfect ending to a perfect day.

That night, four excited sailors recounted their voyage to Mama and John. After she heard us all tell of our discoveries, she said, "Well, this sounds like a day you won't soon forget!" We all nodded.

"We got to see a breach!" repeated Jesse.

"We saw lotsa footprints!" cheered Joy.

"We got to be with Daddy all day!" came the rejoicing of Jeffrey.

And with that comment all the sailors hugged one an-other and created their own sea.

11

Union
Spy
Station

The Whale Watch was a real turning point for me.

The ecstasy of being involved in even the smallest way with the kids was addicting. I so enjoyed watching their faces light up at the discoveries they were making in the educational process. I knew if I could just help out a little more, it would be more than rewarding to me, it would also mean a great deal to Rhonda.

The pregnancy was really taking its toll. The first pregnancy had her total concentration. The second had to be shared with Baby Joy. The third was split between Joy and Jesse. The fourth was divided among three kids plus a move from the East Coast to the West Coast. This fifth one was almost overshadowed by the task of raising four little fireballs.

Yes, the pregnancy was taking its toll all right. Rhonda looked tired. The sparkle in her eye had long since diminished. She was short-tempered and emotional.

She was exhausted.

"Every time I turn my attention to the schooling, we fall behind in keeping the house clean. But when I keep up with my cleaning, we get behind in our schedule of subjects. I fight those two issues constantly, not to mention our desire to fix up the house by painting and carpentry we thought we could do." At this point she would dissolve into tears. "I never know if I'm doing this schooling stuff the right way," she sobbed. "I teach and one day I feel like I'm too heavy into academics, and then another day I feel I've been too lenient."

As I held her, I knew we had to make some changes. "I'm not sure what it is that I could do," I began weakly, "but if I could help you, I'd sure like to do it."

She looked up at me with those big wet eyes and glistening cheeks. "You'd really help?"

"Sure," I responded.

"You're not just saying those words to make me feel better? You really mean it?"

"Yes, I do."

"Well, I've been thinking of a subject that's real important to our curriculum. I've been hammering away at it myself. But I'd love for you to help us with it. I know the kids would love it too."

"What is it?" I asked with a certain degree of uneasiness.

"It's Bible," came the response.

"Bible?"

"Yes, you know, the Holy Scriptures?"

"Well, of course I know what the Bible is, silly! I mean, what's involved in teaching the Bible curriculum to our children?"

"I think you're a creative guy and you could come up with a super method." She was complimenting me. That always means trouble.

"What have you been doing?"

"I've just been reading to them from Proverbs, but I know you can get more creative than that!"

This surfaced a long-standing issue in Union Station. We are very much interested in rearing our children in a strong Christian heritage. Rhonda and I are firm believers in the power that comes from our personal relationship with our God. We also believe the little phrase that comes from Psalms 127:1: "Unless the Lord builds the house, they labor in vain who build it. . . ." We want God to have His proper place in our lives, our home, and now, our curriculum.

Rhonda and I were reaffirmed in this issue by a tidbit she read from Susan Schaeffer Macaulay:

> We ourselves are fellow sheep. We shouldn't act as if we ourselves are the source material for the child. We are to put the child into direct contact with the one who communicated with us.
>
> The expressed knowledge attainable by us has its source in the Bible, and perhaps we cannot do a greater indignity to children than to substitute our own or some other benevolent person's rendering for the fine English, poetic diction, and lucid statement of the Bible.
>
> So we need not necessarily produce "religious" material for the curriculum. It is simple and right to include the reading of Scripture in the daily plan, both at home and/or at school.

Yes, spiritual teaching is important at our place.

But, like so many other dads, I have always felt that I've fallen short in this regard. It's been so much easier to say those words, yet pass the responsibility over to the church. After all, isn't that what Sunday school is all about?

So, Union Station has been very sporadic in its cultivation of religious heritage. In other words, Dad's been inconsistent.

Frankly, if it hadn't been for Rhonda, the kids might have turned out ignorant of these issues. Now she was passing the baton to me, where it rightly belonged in the first place.

What transpired over the next few weeks was a miracle: Rhonda and I gave birth! Not to a baby (although Rhonda would have delivered right then and there if it had been physically possible); we gave birth to a bouncing-baby Bible curriculum!

I refer to it as a miracle because of the way we came in contact with two or three different sources that pointed us in the right direction.

The first idea came about through a speaking engagement I had during the first week of February. I was on a panel at a convention in Washington, D.C. One of my fellow panel-people was David Mains from Wheaton, Illinois. Hearing him speak was quite a treat. He obviously had deep spiritual roots. He was very friendly and warm, and I found his manner engaging.

In talking with some people from his organization, I discovered he had a book about a game called "The God-Hunt." I found the game to be the perfect pick to prime the pump for personalizing prayer!

"Okay, gang," I began at dinner the evening I returned, "we're going to start something new tonight!"

The word *new* always arouses curiosity at our place. "We're going to start playing a game called The God-Hunt!"

"Is it like Candy Land?" asked John.

"No, Johnny, it's a little different. Here's how it works. How many of you know that God is in your life?"

Everyone at the table raised their hands.

"How do you know?"

" 'Cause we have Jesus living inside of us," responded Jeffrey.

"That's right," I affirmed. "Now, do you see God working in your life every day?"

They slowly nodded. In our house slowly nodding means they know they are supposed to be nodding yes but they really mean no.

"Well, The God-Hunt will help you find God every day in your life. Do you all know how to play Hide and Seek?"

"YEAH!" they cheered.

"When you find the person who is hiding—let's say it's Joy—what do you say?"

"I SPY JOY BEHIND THE LIVING ROOM SOFA!!" shouted Jesse.

"Correct!" I responded. "We do the same with God. When we see Him working in our lives we say 'I spy!' "

The kids were excited, but still a little cloudy on this great new game.

"Okay," I continued, "here's how we see God work in our lives. There are four different ways: First, when God answers one of your prayers, that's an 'I Spy.' Second, when you notice something special that shows God taking care of you, that's an 'I Spy.' Third, when there is some unusual or special link or timing, that's an 'I Spy.' And finally, when you feel God helping you do good things in the world for Him, that's an 'I Spy.' "

I felt great until John leaned over and whispered to Jeffrey, "What's all that stuff mean?" and Jeffrey just shrugged his shoulders.

"Give us some examples, Bill," suggested Rhonda, really wanting this game to work.

"Good idea!" I encouraged. "Okay, Joy, I heard you pray that Alyson would not go away last weekend, so that she could come over and spent the night Friday. She was here, right?"

"Right," answered Joy.

"That's an answer to prayer!"

"An 'I Spy,' " she cheered.

"Right. Now, John, you rode your skateboard out in the street yesterday and almost got hit by a car. Remember?"

He nodded.

"Well, you *didn't* get hit. It was God's special care that kept you safe!"

"I spy," he muttered, then smiled real big.

"Now, Mama and I were looking for something to help us teach you kids about prayer and the Bible and spiritual things. I went on this trip, met Mr. Mains, and learned about this game. It was this link and timing that brought it all together!"

"I SPY," cheered Rhonda.

"Jesse, you helped Stevie's mom with her little baby the other day at Little League practice. Nobody asked you to do it, you just went over there and helped. She was very impressed. That's doing God's work in the world—helping people."

By now the entire family shouted in unison, "I SPY!"

"So here's what we'll do. Every night at dinner we'll take turns sharing our 'I Spy' discoveries with one another. It will be fun, and we'll also be learning about how God works in our lives every single day."

The change was immediate and significant. Each evening we'd come to the dinner table and excitedly share our discoveries. Talk went beyond the weather, the terrorists, and the Lakers.

We were talking about God.

We were "I Spying" all over the place. The kids were

coming up with accounts of God at work in their lives in ways that indicated this was more than a game, it was for real. Thank you, David Mains, for starting off our Bible curriculum.

So, a man from Wheaton, Illinois, got the ball rolling. And a short time later a man from Miami, Florida, would pick it up from there.

"How can I share portions of the Bible with the kids in a memorable way?" is the question I asked Rhonda night after night. As we wrestled with the question, we eventually turned to the topic "Who have we seen do this sort of thing effectively?" Our minds flashed back to our college days, when we were dating and only giggling about family.

Phil Myers.

"Why didn't I think of him earlier?" I said, hitting the side of my head. "Remember the evening we went over to their apartment for dinner?"

We both remembered it well. Phil loves kids. To prove it, he has lots of them. Last time I heard, he and his wife, Kay, were up to seven. Anyway, Phil was a professor at the college Rhonda and I attended. He taught a class called Child Growth and Development which was our first exposure to his contagious passion for kids. He invited Rhonda and me to his place for dinner and a show. What a great show it was, too.

After dinner, Phil pulled out a Bible, a tray of colored markers, and a stack of three-by-five-inch index cards. He sat his kids down (I think they had three at the time) and read aloud a brief story from the life of Christ. Then he turned to his markers and drew a picture, together with his kids, of an important moment in the story. The kids were still within their attention span. It only took a few minutes. But what magic minutes.

Later that evening, Phil and Kay showed us a wall in

their apartment that was strung with clothesline. Each index card was hung from the line with a small clothespin. The kids could talk their way through the life of Christ with no help other than the pictures on the cards.

As we came back to the present situation at Union Station, I blurted out to Rhonda: "It's a great idea, but there's one minor hitch."

"What's that?"

"I can't draw."

Rhonda sat in silence. She knew I was right. "The older kids draw better than I do," I lamented.

"Then let's use the kids' drawings!" she replied excitedly. "You read the Bible story and let the four kids each draw their own picture."

I had my confidence back. "That'll work! I can read!" I smiled a smile of security. "I can read *well*, too!" Rhonda patted me on the head. It feels good to do something well.

The next evening we all sat down to dinner and, as usual, the "I Spys" started to fly.

"I prayed that Mama would have a good day and not be sick, and it worked. I spy!" The opening "I spy" was from Jeffrey.

"I got to help Alyson's mama with her cleaning," said Joy. "I spy!"

John got to where he was in somewhat of a rut. He kept announcing the same thing. "God saved my life again today. I spy!"

I raised my eyebrows. "What happened today, John?"

"Oh, a dumb ol' truck was out on the street while I was skateboarding. But you know what? I didn't get killed. I saw it coming and got back on the sidewalk where I belonged."

"Well, if God kept you alive, I guess that's an obvious answer to my prayers, so I spy," I commented while we all smiled.

After dinner I asked everyone to get a piece of paper and some crayons and meet me in the family room. They scurried off while I walked over to get my Bible. I turned to the Gospel of John. I had already decided to read the account of Jesus turning the water into wine. It was short, graphic, and filled with potential.

"Okay, boys and girls," I announced from my seat in the rocking chair, "I'm going to read you a story about Jesus from the Bible. I want you to listen very carefully and when it's over, I want you to draw a picture of an important part of the story, okay?"

They nodded and prepared their positions around the coffee table.

"All right, here we go." I started reading.

> And on the third day there was a wedding in Cana of Galilee; and the mother of Jesus was there;
>
> And Jesus also was invited, and His disciples, to the wedding.
>
> And when the wine gave out, the mother of Jesus said to Him, "They have no wine."
>
> And Jesus said to her, "Woman, what do I have to do with you? My hour has not yet come."
>
> His mother said to the servants, "Whatever He says to you, do it."
>
> Now there were six stone waterpots set there for the Jewish custom of purification, containing twenty or thirty gallons each.
>
> Jesus said to them, "Fill the waterpots with water." And they filled them up to the brim.
>
> And He said to them, "Draw some out now, and take it to the headwaiter," And they took it to him.
>
> And when the headwaiter tasted the water which had become wine, and did not know where it came from (but the servants who had drawn the water knew), the headwaiter called the bridegroom.
>
> And said to him, "Every man serves the good wine

first, and when men have drunk freely, then that
which is poorer; you have kept the good wine until
now."

This beginning of His signs Jesus did in Cana of
Galilee, and manifested His glory, and His disciples
believed in Him.

John 2:1–11

I looked at the kids. They were already well into their
drawings. Rhonda and I watched a wonderful sight. The
kids were in tune to the story. It wasn't a stuffy, boring
old Bible. It was God's Book that lives. We could see its
life in the lives of our four.

Joy finished first. She brought her drawing over to me.
Rhonda suggested, "Tell Daddy what it is that you drew
and how it fits into the story." Then Rhonda looked at me
and said, "I just read a book on this technique. It's called
graphic narration. It's a marvelous way to get the old
creative juices flowing in the mind of a child."

I smiled. "I'm all for creative juices! Tell me what you
have here, Joy."

"Well, Daddy, these are the six pots of water sitting
there getting all ready to be turned into wine by Jesus!"
She was proud of her work and so was I.

I hugged her and kissed her and yelled, "Who's next?"

"Me," came the answer from John. He walked over and
handed me his artwork. "Do you know what, Dad? This is
Jesus over here and He's telling this guy here to go and
get some water."

It was a great drawing. Jesus was green, the servant
was red, and the pots were both green and red.

"Thank you, Johnny. Very good job!" I hugged and
kissed him as well.

"I'm done!" declared Jesse as he brought over his work

and put it on my lap. "This guy is the servant and he's giving the waiter the water that Jesus turned into wine!" He looked up, searching for my approval.

"Great stuff, son!" I grabbed him, kissed him, and hugged him.

"Okay, Jeffrey, let's see what you have." Jeffrey walked over and handed me his drawing. I immediately observed a greater amount of detail to his work. *This little guy has a flair for art,* I thought. He began to explain his creation.

"Here's the bride, here's the groom, and here's the wedding cake," he began. "And this guy in the middle is the guy who finds out that they're all out of champagne!"

I smiled. *Champagne?* I mused. *I guess he figures nothing but the best for God!* I reached over, hugged him, and kissed him.

Well, "I Spy" and drawing pictures have certainly added new dimensions to Union Station Education. Has this enhanced the education of our children? No question about it. How can a Christian possibly think of time in God's Word as anything but enhancement?

Are the kids benefitting? You bet! God is real and vitally involved in their lives. They are *talking* about God at work in their lives, Yes, kids talking about God. It boggles my mind, and it makes me grateful to Him.

The Bible tells us that God's Word will not return void. It's working, even today, even at Union Station!

But I also need to add that we're still struggling with the same old stuff. We're still not as consistent as we'd like to be. We're still feeling pressed by demands that take us away from important things. We're still learning to do more and more looking for God.

And we're improving. We're better off now than we

were a year ago. We needed something to bring the Bible into focus for our family, and we found it. It's an obvious answer to prayer. God spoke to us through Wheaton, Illinois, and Miami, Florida.

"I SPY!"

12

An Abrupt Ending

The pounding on our front door was rather strong. Someone wanted our attention in an intense way. Rhonda walked quickly over to the noise while I sat quietly behind the newspaper.

When Rhonda opened the door, we were both surprised to see one of our neighbors. Surprised, because this gal was always very gentle and sweet—nothing like the knock we heard at the door.

"Hello, Rhonda," she began. I realized I was out of her line of vision. I could see her and hear her, but she couldn't see me.

"Hi, Gloria!" Rhonda replied cheerfully. "Come in and sit down, please."

"No, I can't stay long." She seemed very formal, businesslike, and extremely uncomfortable.

"Well, all right, what can we do for you?" Rhonda was trying her best to make a tense situation tolerable.

Gloria drew a large breath and deliberately stated, "I have noticed something very strange going on with this family for several months now. I finally got up the courage to come over here and talk with you, in hopes that we won't need to bring in the local authorities."

Even though I was carefully concealed behind my newspaper, I slumped down in my chair and further surrounded myself with the sports page. *It's finally happened,* I thought. *I've heard these gory stories of neighbors reporting home-schoolers as truants. They put the kids back in public schools and throw the fathers into the slammer.*

I had a queasy feeling in my stomach. At that moment I realized how fortunate we had been all these months. Our neighbors had their normal questions and curiosities when Union Station Education opened up, but all in all they'd been very open to the concept. I never felt they were offended, and I certainly never felt they'd call the police on us.

But Gloria's face was pale from the seriousness of the matter. She was confronting us with a definite agenda. I stayed behind my newspaper, glancing from side to side, from one wrist to another, wondering if they made handcuffs with enough chain between the cuffs to hold open a copy of the *Los Angeles Times*.

My mind raced to what the *Times* would say when they covered this story, but before I could even design a headline, Rhonda's voice interrupted my thoughts.

"Gloria, please sit down. I don't know exactly what it is that you're describing as strange, but if we could talk it through, I think we'd all feel much better."

"Well, it has to do with your children," she started, in somewhat calmer tones.

I slouched down even farther. I was buried behind my

sports page, mumbling a string of old clichés descriptive of the moment: "The party's over; the gig is up; turn in your key; grab your hat; checkout time; you're history." Fortunately, it went unnoticed.

"Have the kids done something to offend you?" Rhonda asked.

"Well," Gloria stammered. "Yes, in a way."

"In what way?" Rhonda persisted.

"Well, well . . . well, they're not like other children on this block!" she blurted out.

I groaned. "No one else home-schools," I mused. "I'm dead meat."

"Now, Gloria, can you be more specific? Exactly what is the problem?" Rhonda was growing impatient with Gloria's stalling.

I was all ready for Gloria's answer. I was braced for the words *home-schooling* to spew from her mouth in a degrading manner. Gloria leaned forward and touched Rhonda's shoulder. She was ready to pronounce judgment.

"Rhonda, your children have frogs."

There was silence. The only sound in the room was the blinking of eyelashes.

"Frogs?" Rhonda replied in unbelief.

"Frogs." Gloria pointed toward the backyard. "Lots of them. In the back. It's terrible." She stopped to watch Rhonda squirm.

"I-I-I-I don't know what to say!"

"Well, say something!" Gloria pressed. "They're a nuisance to the neighborhood—the frogs, that is—they keep Gerald and me up all night with their croaking and all kinds of commotion! We want something done about it!"

It was time for me to come out of hiding. I put down the newspaper and shuffled over to the couch where Rhonda and Gloria were sitting.

"Hi, gals! Couldn't help but overhear the problem of

141

the frogs. You know what, Gloria? You're right! Those frogs keep me up at night too!"

Rhonda turned sharply and glared at me. "Bill, the kids aren't keeping frogs in the backyard."

"I know," I replied smugly. "But I wanted to let Gloria know that there are frogs back there, however."

Gloria smiled. Rhonda smouldered.

"And, Gloria," I continued, "there are frogs in *your* backyard keeping *us* awake at night."

Gloria's smile quickly vanished, but turned up immediately on Rhonda's face. It was time for a serious explanation.

"You see, Gloria, it's spring, the time of year that those little harmless frogs are all around our neighborhood. Thank goodness they're not the big old bullfrogs, or we'd never get any sleep. But I assure you, the kids aren't raising frogs in our backyard. You're welcome to look back there if you'd care to. We have nothing to hide."

"I guess that won't be necessary," Gloria replied softly. "I'm a little embarrassed by all this. It's just that it always sounded like it was coming from your place and with *all* those kids of yours, I guess I just assumed that ... well, you know what I mean."

Rhonda put her arm around Gloria and squeezed her. "Sure, we understand. Don't be embarrassed. It was an honest mistake."

Gloria smiled, chitchatted for a few more minutes, and went back over to her place to explain the neighborhood's plague of frogs to her husband, Gerald.

"Boy, that was a close one." I sighed.

"What do you mean?" Rhonda asked.

"I thought she was going to blow the whistle on Union Station Education!"

"No, not at all," Rhonda replied matter-of-factly. "Gloria knows what we're doing and she respects us. She has no intention of doing it herself, but she's not going to fly off the deep end and report us, either."

"Well, that's good to know," I said, mostly in an attempt to reassure myself. "You know we *are* legally protected through the Independent Study Program. We're like an extension or satellite campus."

Rhonda smiled. "Do you feel better now that you've heard yourself say those things?" I nodded sheepishly.

"I guess I was kind of reassuring myself," I bashfully replied.

That evening at dinner we checked out some "I Spy" incidents from everyone, and then Rhonda and I recounted the tale of the frogs for the kids. By the end of the story, their eyes were wide with curiosity and interest.

"There's really frogs in our backyard, Daddy?"

"Yes, dozens of them. Don't you hear them at night?"

They all shook their heads. Joy responded, "I always thought that was John snoring with his thumb in his mouth. Holding his blanket!"

Jesse turned his attention to Rhonda. "Mama, can we catch some frogs and keep them in our backyard as pets?"

Rhonda looked less than excited.

"We could make it like part of our science stuff. We could study them."

I decided to let Rhonda off the hook. "No, guys, that's not a real good idea. That's why Gloria came over in the first place. We don't need to make trouble."

Much to my surprise, Rhonda countered my argument. "Wait, Bill. You know, the frogs don't make noise during the day. And you said yourself we have dozens in our backyard. So if we cleared them a nice area, it might be fun and educational to observe a few."

The kids cheered. At Union Station, when you win over Mama, you've won.

When I came home from work the next day, I didn't

even recognize our backyard. I felt like I needed an "E" ticket to Disneyland. I was entering Frog World.

The first thing I noticed in what used to be my backyard was the section over by the garage. We have always felt it was boring to have a yard completely covered with thick, rich, green grass. We are not boring. We have big spots of yard with nothing but dirt. Behind the garage is a fine example of a grassless area.

As I looked at the ground behind the garage, my jaw dropped. Jesse nervously volunteered some information. "Remember, Dad, frogs like water!"

It was no longer a dirt area. It was a mud bowl.

"Hi, Daddy, isn't it great!" came the voices of three more children, all brown, but vaguely familiar.

"Kids?" I mumbled. "Are you my kids?"

"Sure, Daddy! We're a little muddy, but Mama's gonna hose us down before we come back in the house. We went in once already ... now we know not to do that anymore."

I shook uncontrollably, my mind's eye focusing in on what the inside of our house must look like if these mudpies with legs had already visited.

"Oh, hi, dear!" Rhonda spoke sweetly as she scurried out the back door. "I had hoped to catch you before you got back here!"

"To warn me?"

"No, no, silly," said Rhonda, still trying to play down Mud Mountain. "To *share* with you the excitement of our science project."

I forced a feeble smile.

"What have we learned today, kids?" Rhonda pushed on, not wanting to leave room for me to explode.

"Frogs are fast!" yelled Jeffrey.

"Frogs like to be around stuff with the same color as

they are, so they blend in and you can't see them!" volunteered Joy.

"Yeah, Dad, here's my favorite frog." Jesse beamed as he pulled his right hand out from behind his back to offer me his own personal choice for Finest Frog of Frog World. He caught me off guard, so I jumped back when suddenly eyeball to eyeball with this toad.

"Don't be scared, Dad, they don't hurt!"

Jesse's consoling only embarrassed me, so I started turning red. "I'm not afraid," I snapped. "I'm no sissy."

I was still embarrassed and flushed, but Jesse went right on. "Dad, I want you to meet my own personal frog. His name is Flash Gordon Camouflage. You can just call him Flash."

"Flash Gordon 'cause he's fast, Dad," explained Jeffrey, as if the name was a mystery.

"And that last name—however you say it—'cause he blends in with the mud," ventured John, clearly unable to yet pronounce *camouflage*.

I was still in shock over the mud. "But look at this part of the yard," I begged, pointing to the area in question. "It's all mud!"

"Mama wouldn't let us muddy up the whole yard," Jesse responded, totally missing the point. "So I'm sorry we could only use this one section."

Rhonda grabbed my arm and began touring me through Frog World. "Here's the water in the shade. Here's the water in the sunlight. Here's some rocks for our frog friends to sit on during the day. Isn't it a wonderful little project, sweetie?"

"Little?" I peeped. "Let's take down the fences and let these frogs have their freedom."

"Oh, don't be silly!" Rhonda scoffed and walked over to the hose to begin the process of cleaning. As she turned on the faucet, I couldn't resist a little scoffing of my own.

"You mean to tell me there's a child somewhere in that pile of mud?" I followed up my sarcastic question with a cynical laugh. But I learned a valuable lesson:

Never be sarcastic when your wife is holding a hose.

The next day I spent a lot of my time at the office working on my attitude. I didn't want to be a drawback to the science division of Union Station Education. I gave myself a serious talking to, and when I drove up the driveway that evening, I was a different Daddy.

I bounded out of the car, rubbed my hands together in joyous anticipation, and shouted, "Where are those toads? Let me back into Frog World!"

I was pleased with my enthusiasm. I was genuine. I wasn't manufacturing anything. Science was never my strong suit in school, so maybe *I* could learn something this time around.

As I opened the fence gate leading to the backyard, it was immediately evident that something was wrong.

Frog World was gone.

The rocks were cleared, the mud was covered over with dry dust, now somewhat damp. All the barriers were removed. There were no frogs.

I turned around and walked into the house. The normal hustle and bustle of Union Station was missing. There was an eerie silence that could be cut with a knife.

"Hi, Daddy," came a mournful greeting from Joy. Her eyes were red from crying. "We let all our frogs go today."

"I see," I said softly. "Why did we let all our frogs go today?"

"Jesse had an accident with a baby frog," she whispered. She could hardly complete the sentence without crying. She ran back into her room.

Rhonda came out of the kitchen at that point. We

hugged and she spoke softly in my ear. "You need to talk with Jesse. He's very upset. I think he really needs you right now."

"What happened?"

"Let him tell you."

So I quietly and quickly walked down the hall toward Jesse's bedroom. There were sobs from behind every door. I knocked. "Jesse, may I come in?"

The door opened, and a tear-stained face immediately buried itself in my chest. "Daddy, Daddy, I did a terrible, awful thing. I didn't mean to. I meant to do what you said. Oh, I'm so sorry, Daddy."

I held him in silence for several minutes, in hopes he would settle down enough to tell me the details that still escaped me. After a few minutes he seemed in control.

"Now Jesse, just relax. Tell me exactly what happened."

He swallowed hard. His eyes welled up again with tears. He spoke slowly.

"Well, I went out back this morning to see Flash Gordon Camouflage . . . and I . . . and I saw this little baby frog all by himself. He looked—he looked lonely and sad, Daddy." He put his head down and we hugged again for a minute.

"Go on, son, tell me more."

"Well, I remember . . . last night—last night you said something to Mama about letting these frogs have their freedom. He looked so sad, Daddy, so . . . so . . . ." He swallowed hard again. "So I took the baby frog and put him out behind our yard in the alley, you know, so he could get his freedom. He didn't move, he just stayed still. I figured he wasn't moving 'cause I was still there . . . so I left."

"Did you tell Mama you did this?"

His head dropped again and he couldn't speak. He only shook it.

"Okay, now tell me what happened."

He lifted his head and continued in choked-up tones. "I forgot about the baby frog for the rest of the day . . . I thought he was happy because he was free. Right after lunch I remembered him, so I ran out to the alley to be sure he was happy—or gone—but he was still there in the alley." He reached for me and I hugged him again, very tightly. The hugging muffled his voice, but the words still rang true.

"He's dead, Daddy—the baby frog is dead. I killed him. He needed shade. He died in the sun. There was no water . . . I didn't mean to, I'm so sorry, Daddy . . . I wanted him to be free."

I continued to hold him close. I felt so bad for him. He had nothing but purity in his motives and yet he had to face an abrupt change in direction.

Jesse went into the bathroom to wash his face with cold water. I went out to talk with Rhonda.

"You can see how upset he is," she whispered. "It seemed like the best thing to do was let all the frogs go back to wherever they came from. We cleaned it all up late this afternoon."

I nodded in agreement. "It still was a good idea, though," I commented. "It brought frogs out of the science book and right into life itself."

My last comment caught Rhonda in an unusual way. She looked off, beyond me, for several minutes. Finally she commented, "Since we brought frogs out of the science book and right into life, we gained an unexpected dimension. Since we brought frogs to life, we had to deal with death as well."

Dinner was quiet at Union Station that evening. It was a night to be alone with your thoughts.

13

Taking a
Peek at
Being Unique

The summer months became quite inflating.

Rhonda was coming down to the wire on this pregnancy, and she was becoming increasingly uncomfortable as she grew in size. The baby was an active one, always kicking, wiggling, turning somersaults, or square dancing.

Nevertheless, Union Station Education continued to go on strong. During June, July, and August, most usually associated with school vacation, Rhonda did her best to keep the kids on their schedule. They had plenty of time for play with their friends in the mornings, after chores. But after lunch, they'd faithfully hit the books.

"Why do I have to do these dumb old spelling words, anyway?" Jesse griped one afternoon. "All the other kids are outside, and I'm in here doing this rotten stuff." He added to this statement his most pained expression, which he rehearsed for hours in front of the bathroom mirror.

"Jesse, that's a good question to ask, and I want to give you an answer," Rhonda replied with empathy. "It doesn't seem fair that the other kids play and you have school, does it?"

Jesse shook his head.

Rhonda suddenly felt our own Flying Wollenda performing in her tummy. Her eyes sparkled. "Well, let me show you one very good reason why we're pushing so hard on your schooling this summer." At that, she reached for Jesse's hand and gently placed it on her multidirectional belly.

"I felt the baby kick!" screamed the delighted older brother.

"You've got that right!" Rhonda echoed. "And do you know what? It will only be a few more days before that little baby makes an entrance into this world."

Jesse smiled broadly. Like his sister and other brothers, he did not see a new baby as an intruder, but as a welcomed family member.

"But here's the issue, Jess," Rhonda went on. "When the baby arrives, things are going to slow down around here. School will be one of the things that slows down— a lot."

" 'Cause you need time to take care of the baby and you need time to rest," Jesse finished the thought, now realizing he had heard this before.

"Correct. So when everyone else is back in school, you'll have some time off. You're getting vacation; you're just getting it later than the other kids."

Jesse grinned and put his hand back on Rhonda's tummy. "Okay, Mama, I'll do my spelling words."

His timing was perfect, for just as he returned to his workbook, the phone rang.

"Rhonda? Hi, this is Debbie McIntire. How's my favorite pregnant person?"

"Big," was my wife's one-word commentary on pregnancy.

"Well, I'm just calling to remind you that this Saturday will be orientation for our new home-school parents in the Independent Study Program. Are you and Bill planning on attending?"

"Yes, unless I'm in labor."

"Great. Would you and Bill like to be on a panel discussion about some of your methods in home-schooling?"

"What do you mean?" Rhonda asked, gradually panicking.

"I was thinking of certain curriculum ideas that you use that are effective. Like the presidents, for instance. I think that's a great way to learn history. I'd love for the other parents to be exposed to those sorts of creative ideas."

"Uhh, well, okay, Debbie, I'll talk to Bill. . . ."

"Wonderful. I'll put you down on the list. We'll see you Saturday."

"Unless I'm in labor," Rhonda added.

"Bye-bye!"

"Please, God, let me be in labor," Rhonda muttered when she realized Debbie had already hung up. "I hate panels."

A person who hates panels with the equal intensity of his wife arrived home from work that evening only to be greeted with the news.

"Hi. This Saturday we're on a panel about home-schooling up at the Independent Study Program's orientation meeting. The only way we can get out of it is to throw me into labor. Got any ideas?"

I stood there in the doorway and blinked.

"There you go, blinking again. Get inside the house

and use some of that blinking energy to help us figure out what we're going to do!"

I walked in, sat down, and had her recount her phone conversation with Debbie.

"I hate panels," I announced. "Quick, pack your bags, we're leaving the country."

"No good," Rhonda quipped. "In the first place, that's an awful expensive excuse to get out of panel discussions. In the second place, I already called the airlines and they won't let me fly this close to my due date."

"Well, it looks like we're on," I succumbed to the inevitable conclusion.

"I see Dr. Davis tomorrow," volunteered my sweetie. "Maybe he'll hospitalize me Saturday."

I looked at her as if to say, "You don't really believe that, do you?"

"It's a thought," came her weak reply.

Next morning it was down the road to the office of Dr. Davis. Even though he's an obstetrician, his waiting room isn't exactly suited for four children. They painstakingly read through *McCall's, Vogue,* and *Woman's Day.* The lone copy of *Highlights for Children* was damaged beyond recognition, apparently a result of a fight over it by a previous group of youngsters.

"Rhonda," the nurse called her. "Come into Room B; Dr. Davis will be right with you."

The kids looked at Mama to see if this would be a visit where they could come in with her. An earlier visit gave them the opportunity to learn more about the *inside* of a doctor's office.

"Not this time, kids," Rhonda apologized. "Wait quietly out here. I'll be out in a minute."

The kids obeyed, but in quite a dejected manner. They were imprisoned in a room with nothing but women's magazines. It was a sadistic scene.

Dr. Davis greeted Rhonda warmly. "Hello, little lady. We're not so little anymore, are we?"

Rhonda smiled. That sort of comment can be bother-some, but not when it comes from your doctor. He went on.

"I see by looking at your file, that you're not too far off from D-day."

"Do you think the baby will arrive this weekend?" Rhonda blurted out.

"Hmm, that's hard to say," he replied. Of course, this being her fifth child, Rhonda knew that a doctor *never* answers that question anyway. "Let me examine you and see if all is well."

His exam was quick and positive. "Everything is just fine. Meet me over in my office across the hall, and let's talk for a few minutes." He went to another examination room, while Rhonda waited patiently for him in his office. He finally entered and sat down across the desk from her.

"Rhonda, pregnancy is a miraculous experience," he began. "In many respects, all pregnancies are alike. The same basic functions take place in all expectant mothers. But"—he paused for added contrast—"in many respects each pregnancy is a unique experience. Each woman has her own distinct manner. And even a woman like your-self, who is ready to give birth a fifth time, must realize that each of your four previous births were unique in their own way."

"You're right," Rhonda interjected. "They were all long and painful, but each one was unique in its own special way."

"Exactly. Now, I've been reviewing your file. Looking back over your other four births, you clearly illustrate a woman's unique approach to delivery."

"What do you mean?" Rhonda asked.

"I'm referring to your uterus."

"Oh yeah, that dumb thing," she replied with tones of mock disgust.

"Your uterus is somewhat faulty," Dr. Davis continued in his speech. His voice was a pleasant mix of empathy and matter-of-factness. "When you have contractions, you should have a push down." He demonstrated a downward motion with his hands. "But your uterus doesn't exactly do that. It's more of a push *in,* in your case. So, we're looking at a much longer labor."

"But everything's okay, right?" Rhonda suddenly felt the need for comfort.

"There should be no problem," the doctor consoled. "You're just unique, that's all." He smiled a reassuring smile. "So, take care and I'll see you next week," he concluded as he rose from his chair, "or sooner in the labor room of the hospital!" He winked.

Rhonda gathered up the kids and headed back to Union Station. She phoned me at the office to let me know about the chat she had with Dr. Davis. She was in remarkably good spirits, however. She ended our phone call with a barb.

"A faulty uterus and a panel discussion. What a heavy cross it is that I must bear!"

Much to our chagrin, Saturday arrived but the baby didn't.

We drove up to the school in silence. Our minds were flooded with thoughts. Inwardly, I battled with myself:

I hate panels.

This could be a very profitable time.

I could be home with the kids.

This time will hold some valuable lessons for Rhonda and me.

I hate panels.

We'll be better home-school parents because we're going today.

The battle raged on. Yet, before we knew what was happening, the car was in the school's parking lot. We squeezed each other's hand as a signal of our team spirit. We both took a deep breath and walked into the meeting room.

As in most meetings of this sort, all the guys ended up over by the coffeepot, waiting for the meeting to begin, nervously small-talking about this year's chances for the Rams and the Raiders. The women were in the opposite corner of the room, talking babies. They had sort of surrounded Rhonda, obviously the one closest to baby time.

"How do you feel, Rhonda?" asked a concerned mother.

"Like a beached whale," responded a woman twice her normal size. "If I don't have this baby soon, I'm going to burst!"

This led to a rousing revival of previous birth accounts by the other mothers. One particularly zealous mother was about ready to show battle scars—her stretch marks—when Debbie called the meeting to order.

"We have a full schedule of events planned for today, so let's go ahead and begin!"

When Debbie promised a full schedule, it became quickly apparent she was a woman of her word. We had motivational talks, educational talks, goal-setting sessions, introductions to curriculum, calendar overview, introductions to field trips, how to keep compulsory attendance sheets for the state of California, and the presentation of a gift for each set of parents.

"I have an apple for each teacher," Debbie laughed and held one high for all to see. "But home-schooling is tough, so you'll notice each apple has a special attachment." She turned over the piece of fruit to reveal a small white tablet taped to its side.

"An aspirin," she stated, "for those times when an ap-

ple is not enough." We all laughed, partly at the thought-
ful piece of humor but mostly at its truth.

"Let's take a little break and then we'll have our panel
discussion."

This break was far less relaxed than the first one.
Rhonda and I took a walk outside, hand in hand. That
way, one of us couldn't run off. Before we went back in, I
turned her toward me and looked her straight in the eye.
"Rhonda," I began, "I just want to tell you that it's not too
late to go into labor." I paused. "You may begin."

Well, she didn't.

So we were up in front of this group of folks with three
other couples, the Williamses, the Sandersons, and the
Huffmans. Debbie served as moderator. She started right
in on us.

"Rhonda, tell us some of the unique facets of the
Butterworths' home-schooling."

Rhonda nervously plowed through a president a week,
Heppie Bread, and aaa, aaa, apple.

"Wonderful. Laura, tell us about school at the Williams
house."

Laura went through their family variations: one of the
United States each week, a superduper reading program,
and some exciting science projects.

Debbie went right down the line, allowing each family
to put their best foot forward in their respective areas of
strength.

But as the panel went on, there was an increase in
variety. The degree of difference was displayed with each
additional question.

The Sandersons work from elaborate lesson plans, the
Butterworths use a much simpler model. The Huffmans
give grades and tests, the Williamses don't give grades,
the Sandersons don't give either. We teach in the afternoon, the others teach in the morning. Bob Huffman

teaches science and social studies, Mike Sanderson doesn't teach at all. The Huffmans stress academics, the Williamses stress chores, domestic duties, and "life-related experiences."

Needless to say, heads were spinning as the panel perspired through their forty-five minutes of presentation. When the discussion ended, so did the day's activities.

"Thank you all for coming," Debbie concluded. "I hope this has been a day of stimulation for you. Have a great year of home-schooling!"

As Rhonda and I drove home, we debriefed from the day.

"How do you feel?" I asked her.

"Oh, the normal feelings: guilty, depressed, and like a failure."

"I see," I commented softly.

"There are *so* many things I want to do with home-schooling. Lots of the ideas that were shared are good ones, but how do I pull it all off? Where can I find the time to develop other aspects of our curriculum? I know that session was supposed to be encouraging, but I feel under the pile."

"You *are* doing a good job, babe."

"I guess. Sometimes I just don't know."

"There are a lot of different methods out there. We experiment and find what works for our crew and we go with it."

All of a sudden, without warning, Rhonda appeared to totally shift gears in our topic of conversation. She yelled at the top of her voice: "PREGNANCY!"

I just about drove off the road. "Is it time? Should I head us to the hospital?"

"No, no, it's not time yet," she replied, once again in control of her composure. "I was just thinking about what Dr. Davis said the other day about pregnancy." She paused and added, "Home-schooling and pregnancy are a lot alike."

This ought to be interesting, I thought. "How's that?" I said aloud.

"In lots of ways, home-schooling is the same in each home. There are basic functions that need to take place. But each home school is unique. We will conduct our school differently from the Williamses or the Sandersons or even Debbie, if she had her own home school."

"I think I understand what you're saying," I encouraged. Before I could go on, she came back with the statement to bring things together.

"Just as each pregnancy is unique, so each home school is unique. Not better or worse, necessarily—just unique."

I could see in her face that the battle with guilt and failure wasn't finished. No, that war would rage on. I wonder, is it ever over? But as we pulled into the driveway of Union Station, Rhonda was in a positive frame of mind. We walked in to find the house in its usual state after being in the hands of a baby-sitter for seven hours.

I untied the sitter and offered to drive her home. She accepted my invitation. All the kids were out playing, with the exception of Jesse. He took this opportunity to find out about the day from Mama.

"Where did you guys go today, Mom?"

"Oh, we went to a meeting about home-schooling," Rhonda replied, busy cleaning up the kitchen.

"Was it just you and Daddy?"

"No, there were several moms and dads with kids learning at home."

"Was it fun?"

"It was *interesting*," Rhonda stated emphatically.

"Does that mean it wasn't fun?"

"No, it means we learned a lot."

158

"What did you learn?" he continued to prod.

"Well, we learned that home-schooling means different things to different people, even people who are involved in home-schooling."

"You mean some people do it different than us?"

"Yes, that's what I mean. It doesn't mean Union Station Education is better than the rest or worse than the rest. . . ."

"But it's best for us, right, Mama?"

As he looked up at her, his big eyes searched for the security that only she could provide. Rhonda put down her work, dried her hands, and held her arms out for a big hug from her eldest son.

"Yes, Jesse, Union Station Education is the best we can give you, you special little guy!"

That was all he needed—a little love, a little support, a little security. He started off down the hall toward his bedroom, when he suddenly stopped, turned around, and asked an important question.

"Mama, are you gonna let me go off to college?"

Rhonda smiled and replied, "Yes, Jesse, we'll let you go off to college."

"Whew," was the relieved response of our small wonder, "that's good. 'Cause when I'm that age, it'll be time to start looking for a WIFE and I hear that college is the place to get one!"

He walked off, whistling, leaving Mama shaking her head and mumbling, "That boy is just like his daddy."

14

Now Arriving at Union Station

When God decided not to throw Rhonda into labor and spare us from the panel discussion, I lost the sense of urgency for labor contractions to begin. *The birth can occur whenever*, I thought. *There are no pressing engagements that I need to get out of.*

Rhonda saw the issue in an entirely different light. She wanted the birth, and she wanted it *now!* Because of her faulty uterus, she knew she was in for a long labor, so she began to think about the prize at the other end of the run—a brand-new son or daughter.

Monday morning, two days after the home-school panel, Rhonda called me at the office with important news. Unfortunately, I was preoccupied with a problem at work, so I wasn't doing well at paying attention.

"Bill?"

"Hi, babe!"

"Bill, something is starting to happen."

"What do you mean?"

"Every time the clock strikes the hour, I feel a deep pain in my stomach."

"Well, don't worry. When I get home I'll take a look at that dumb clock."

"BILL!"

"Babe?"

"You're not even listening to me. There's no problem with the clock. I'm starting to have regular contractions, and they are one hour apart!"

"CONTRACTIONS! All right, okay, easy now, relax, I'll pack my briefcase and be home in ten minutes, sit down, put your feet up, do your breathing exercises, get a—"

"Bill, calm down. You don't need to come home. The contractions are an *hour* apart. It's just the beginning."

I hung up the phone and sat in numbness. It was a mixture of excitement, embarrassment, and edginess. The rest of the day was spent staring at the phone. It would occasionally ring, and I'd answer it with such blazing speed, it would never finish its first ring. But the calls weren't from Rhonda. They were from pushy people, presuming that I was at the office to work, and this really bothered me. I'd do my best to sidestep each of them.

"Listen, I'd love to talk about this issue," I'd typically tell them over the phone, "but my wife is in the first stages of labor. I need to keep the phone lines clear so I can get her to the hospital at the right time."

That explanation always worked, but I'd add another tactic just for good measure. "Besides," I'd say, "it's August. Nobody works in August. Everyone is vacationing. It's too hot to work in August."

I came home Monday evening to find the situation was progressing. The contractions were coming every forty-five minutes. The contraction would come; Rhonda would breathe funny; life would go on.

Tuesday at work was a carbon copy of Monday. I was tense, preoccupied, and not much good. When I went home for lunch, Rhonda announced, "The contractions are now coming every thirty minutes. We're making progress!"

We all cheered. The kids were so excited about the birth! Jeffrey pulled me aside before I went back to work, however, and he put it all in perspective for me.

"Dad, Mom needs to have this baby soon. She's been teaching us like crazy, 'cause once this baby comes she'll have to take a break. She's teaching me so much stuff, Dad, my brain is gonna 'splode!"

I patted him on the head and encouraged him to hang in there.

Tuesday's twenty- to thirty-minute gaps led to Wednesday's ten- to fifteen-minute gaps, which gave way to Thursday's five- to ten-minute spacings.

"We're getting close now," she told me as I left for work Thursday morning. "Be encouraged, this could be the day!"

As I was driving to the office, I mused, "Why was *she* encouraging *me*? *She's* the one who's going to have the baby! *I* should be encouraging *her!*"

I called pretty regularly that day. Marilyn, a good friend and neighbor, had come over to offer assistance, so I did most of my talking with her.

"Marilyn, how's she doing?"

"She's doing fine. They're still every five to ten minutes. But they do seem to be getting stronger."

"Okay, I'll call back in a little bit."

A little bit would go by and I'd be on the phone again.

"Marilyn, what's the word?"

"They're down to five now."

"Let me talk to her."

"Bill?"

"Rhonda, how do you feel?"

"Like I'm having contractions every five to ten minutes."

"What are you doing? Are you resting?"

"No, I'm trying to keep my mind off my labor."

"How?"

"I'm teaching school!"

Sure enough, as the day passed on, I'd call and get Marilyn. But in the background I could hear my little, lovely laborer giving her best shot to Union Station Education.

"Jesse, nine plus eight."

"Seventeen."

"Correct. Nine minus nine."

"Zero."

I'd hear a long pause over the phone.

"Zero, Mama."

More pause.

"Mama? Nine minus nine is zero, right?"

Finally Marilyn would resolve the issue: "Jesse, your Mama's having a contraction right now, so she can't talk real well. But you are right, nine minus nine is zero."

I came home Thursday evening to a chorus of exhaustion. Joy, Jesse, and Jeffrey were waiting for me at the front door.

"Dad, we did Language, Reading, Math, and Spelling all afternoon," Jesse offered as the spokesman for the group. "We need a break—bad. She needs to have the baby. We think tonight would be a good night for it. What do you say, Dad? Are you with us?"

"I'm with you, guys," I smiled, "but it doesn't always work that way." Their faces drooped. "Let's go in and see what progress she's making!" I tried my best at encouragement.

I guess I was starting to get accustomed to labor pains. Thursday night was like Wednesday, Tuesday, and Monday nights: Rhonda would have a contraction, and then try to go back to whatever she was doing.

So when I went to bed Thursday night, I fully expected to get up Friday morning, go to work, keep checking, and go about my business.

I was awakened, not by my alarm clock, but by my alarmed wife.

"Bill, Bill, wake up!"

"Huh?" I grumbled. "Did I oversleep? Did the alarm go off?"

"No, wake up. It's time to go to the hospital!"

Now I was awake.

I glanced at the clock. "Two-forty-five A.M. and I'm gonna be a father!"

"You already are a father, dear," Rhonda countered. "Please dress quickly. We need to go."

Marilyn was already at our house, ready to stay with the other four fast-asleep kiddos.

"Will you be able to wait till we get to the hospital?" I asked in all sincerity.

Rhonda furrowed her brow and gave a half-smile. "My labors are long, Bill. We live six minutes from the hospital. I think I can hold on."

"So that means I don't have to . . ."

"Right, Bill. No speeding through red lights or police escorts to the hospital. Just a nice six-minute drive."

Even in labor, she knew me so well. I had always dreamed of high-speed trips to the hospital. But this would be my fifth leisurely drive.

The next nine hours were spent in the activity that must have inspired the saying "The darkest hour is just before the dawn." A woman really has to work before she gets her baby. The man stands around, pretty helpless, watching this happen to his wife. Labor really zaps her strength, but the only nourishment available is ice. Rhonda ate ice chips like a woman possessed. Work does make a person hungry.

Even the man can get hungry after nine hours in a labor room. But men—don't you dare eat! When Rhonda was in labor with another child of ours, I quietly snuck out and ate four Oreo cookies from a candy machine. I came back in with black teeth, and she has never forgiven me for that injustice. If the woman can't eat, the man can't eat.

Time in a labor room moves at the speed of a glacier. Nine hours seemed like ninety, but the word from Dr. Davis finally arrived.

"Roll her down to Delivery Room A. Mr. Butterworth, put on your hospital garb. You're gonna have your baby real soon."

Like most fathers, I was so excited about going to the delivery room, that I had no idea how utterly ridiculous I looked in a gown, booties, surgical mask, and shower cap. No wonder the first thing babies do is cry.

My honey, my sweetie, was holding up like the true champion she is. Her uterus hadn't disappointed her. She had five days of contractions. But it was heading toward this moment beyond description.

She was in position and pushing hard. We squeezed hands with every push.

"I see the head," Dr. Davis encouraged. "Let's have a few more good pushes, Rhonda."

As the head came in sight, I blurted out, "It looks just like the other four!"

"We'll find out if 'it' is a he or a she," replied the doctor, never looking up from his work.

"Jill or Joseph," mumbled Rhonda, as she continued to push.

"All right, Rhonda. One more hard push."

She gave it her all. Dr. Davis handled the baby expertly. The nurses clapped and cheered while we all looked for the answer to our question.

"Well, hello, Joseph!" Dr. Davis exclaimed. "You appear to be a very healthy little boy!"

There was laughter. There were tears. A nurse held Joseph while Dr. Davis was finishing up with Rhonda.

"Nine pounds, one ounce, twenty-one-and-a-half-inches long!"

"What's his full name?" another nurse asked Rhonda.

"Joseph Morgan Lindsey Butterworth," she said as she smiled with pride.

"A big name for a big boy," the doctor mumbled.

It is a big name, I thought. *It's rich in family tradition and personal significance.*

They brought him over and gently placed him on Rhonda's newly flattened stomach. Each of our five kids were successively bigger at birth. This guy was the bruiser. Watching Rhonda as she held him in her arms for the first time was more than I could handle without tears. I reached down and hugged them both, grateful to observe this beautiful bonding that was taking place.

I stood up again and employed my usual cover for my emotions. I held my nose and did my impression of a public address announcer:

"Ladies and gentlemen, now arriving at Union Station ... Joseph ... Morgan ... Lindsey ... Butterworth ... ALL ABOARD!!"

15

Union Station Evaluation

Joseph's arrival at Union Station not only gave the kids a break from school, it also gave Mama and Daddy a chance to look back and critique the success of this grand experiment. Was home-schooling worth the effort? What changes occurred in the kids? What changes did it make in Rhonda's life? Should we continue? How did we do in individual academic areas?

Questions like these became the second most popular topic at our place. First place was reserved for Joseph. He was turning out to be the ideal fifth child. He was easygoing, usually happy, and quite tolerant of his older brothers and sister.

One Saturday afternoon, Rhonda and I searched for a quiet spot in our house to do a little Union Station evaluation. We started in the dining room, but we were distracted by too much noise in the adjoining family room. We went out in the back to the patio, but that, too, turned out bad. We eventually ended up in our bedroom.

In the kindest of terms, our bedroom was filled with potential. In stark reality, it was a mess.

It was a large room, brightly lit, newly wallpapered in a lovely blue with pink accents. Yet it needed trim around the doors and closets, baseboards, curtains for the window, and moulding in various spots.

However the main problem with talking in our bedroom wasn't noise—it was discomfort. We had our bed, a bureau, and a chest of drawers, but no chairs. This was a holdover from our tiny former house. We had no room for chairs in our bedroom where we used to live. Our new Union Station bedroom had the room, but no chairs.

Rhonda sat on the bed Indian style, and I rattled around in a hundred different positions on the floor.

"Well, babe, after a year of home-schooling, what are your thoughts?" I began the discussion from my spot by the bed.

"It was a tough year," Rhonda started, "but it was well worth it. So many good things came to our lives as a result—look at Joy."

"Where?"

"No. I mean look at Joy as an example of what I'm saying. Before we started this teaching at home, she was really struggling with personal insecurity. But the time, attention, and tender loving care that can be awarded to each child really brought her out of her shell. She's more confident and definitely more secure."

"I agree," I said, while changing positions on the floor. I was now on my back. "I can see how it's helped Jesse, too. The flexibility of a personal tutor really benefitted him. He was slower in math so you had the extra time to bring him along. Thanks to the extra time you were able to give him, his speed has improved significantly."

"And of course the other side of that is giving him room to explore even further in subjects he loves," Rhonda added. "He spent hours with his science kit and all his experiments."

"Don't forget Jeffrey," I reminded. "He couldn't ask for a better start than the year you've given him. Personal instruction in phonics and math, and I love the way you've been able to encourage him in his drawing. Why, he could be another Bil Keane, cartooning his own version of the *Family Circus.*"

At the mention of our favorite comic strip, Rhonda smiled.

"It's been a significant year for everyone," I concluded.

"The change isn't as dramatic in the boys," Rhonda interjected. "But it's still good stuff that's happening through our effort. It's even been of help to John."

I laughed. "Yes, our little Union Station Eavesdropper learned quite a few things by listening in on conversations designed for his older brother."

We paused for a moment, lost in our thoughts. I was the one to start talking. "Well, I guess that settles it. Union Station Education was wonderful." I grinned a big grin.

Rhonda leaned over from her spot on the bed and gave me a big hug. "I love you," she said as she squeezed me. "You amaze me with your ability to reduce things down to simple terms."

I hugged her back. "Yeah, I guess that is pretty amazing."

"But not always accurate."

I pulled away. "What? What is that supposed to mean?" I was getting hot.

"Well, calm down, first of all. I'm just saying that all

we did so far was talk about the positive results of home-schooling. We didn't finish the discussion and you've already pronounced it *wonderful!*"

"Do you have further feelings about this past year?" I asked, mixing politeness with a little cynicism. For you see, my wife, like so many wives, has further feelings on almost any subject.

"Well, yes, I have some more things I want to say," she responded, willing to overlook my taunt. "This entire home-school issue continues to carry a certain degree of frustration with it."

"What do you mean?"

"Take the individual subjects. We had a good year in reading and language. We had an okay year in math. The presidents were marvelous, but we weren't always as consistent as I would have liked to have been. Science was real poor, I felt. And there were so many other subjects I wanted to get to this year! Heppie Bread was a great idea, but when I got pregnant, it shut down the oven."

"But I know you too well, babe. Next year will be different," I encouraged.

"You're right," she conceded. "That's an important point to keep in mind. I guess *every* year I do this, it'll be a little different."

After another long pause I ventured out with one more question: "Was it worth it?"

She didn't even pause to think. "Worth it? Yes, definitely. It was a very worthwhile experience for all of us."

"Good!" I cheered.

"But . . ." she added, "it was not without its price."

"How do you mean that?" I probed.

"Home-schooling cost us this past year. I'm talking about costs beyond the dollars and cents of buying curriculum, paying for the Independent Study Program, and purchasing globes, bulletin boards, and desks. I guess a better word to describe it is *trade-offs*."

"Trade-offs?"

"Yes. This year was a year of trade-offs. We didn't do many things we wanted to do this year. And much of the reason was home-schooling."

"Like what? Give me an example."

"Well, the house is the most obvious one. When we moved into Union Station, we moved into a fixer-upper. We knew it would take lots of work to get it into shape. We've been able to do some work. But much of it has been put on hold because of the extra time demanded by our family."

"Okay, now I see what you're talking about," I concurred.

"Look at our living room," she pressed on. "It's empty! We still haven't put one piece of furniture in our living room!"

I nodded in understanding. Since we had moved from a house with a living room, to a house with a living room *and* a family room, we only had furniture for one room. She was correct. Our living room was a naked testimony to trade-offs.

"Yeah, I guess *trade-offs* is a good word for what's involved," I muttered.

"Fixing up and buying furniture are just a couple of examples," Rhonda continued. "There are a lot of days we trade off with more basic aspects of life. We don't get the house cleaned as often as we'd like. Home-cooked meals from scratch often end up as good intentions. And Mount Saint Dirty Clothes just seems to get higher and higher!"

"Trade-offs?"

"Trade-offs."

"I guess I need to ask again. Was it worth it?"

Rhonda smiled. "It sure was."

"The kids took end-of-the-year tests through the Independent Study Program. They all tested out at grade level or above." I reviewed this information with her for her encouragement.

Rhonda laughed and reached over to a magazine on her nightstand. "I was just reading an article in this magazine about home-schooling. There was an entire section on testing. Just listen to some of these stories." She began to read:

> The Hewitt Research Foundation which specializes in educational research, found that of the families challenged by the courts for teaching at home, the home-school children averaged 30 percent higher on standardized tests than conventionally schooled children.

"I guess it's a good thing our kids did well in the tests!" I laughed.

Rhonda read on:

> In New York State five home-school families were challenged for truancy. The local school superintendent gave their seven children the Stanford Achievement Test. The national average on the test is 50 percent. All seven children scored between 90 and 99 percent.

"Wow!" I exclaimed. "I'm impressed!"
"Here's my favorite," Rhonda remarked.

> In California a family started giving their son formal education at about the age of eight. Much of his curriculum centered on books of his choice from the local library. The father, a social scientist, and mother, an English teacher, were concerned about

their boy's understanding of natural and physical
sciences, subjects the parents knew little about. Last
year, their son, age eighteen, turned down a Yale
offer and accepted a $12,000 scholarship to study
Geology at Harvard. Their sixteen-year-old son is an
amateur astrophysicist and has constructed a twelve-
inch refracting telescope.

"Home-schooler turns down Yale to go to Harvard—
terrific!" I cheered.

"But remember," Rhonda reminded. "Home-schooling
is so much more than school at home. It's bigger than
academics. It's—"

"Total education," I interrupted.

"Exactly," she responded as her eyes lit up. "By George,
I think you've got it!" she said in her best British accent.

I rumpled her hair and continued on the *My Fair Lady*
motif: "You've been a great 'Enry 'Iggins."

She looked out the window. "Yes, this has been quite
an experience, quite a year!" Suddenly her face lost all
color and her eyes widened in a look of fright. "Bill! Do
you know what's coming up in a few weeks?"

"What?" I gasped.

"My birthday!" she moaned. "I'm gonna be thirty!" Her
body went limp and she fell back onto the bed.

"Yes, you've accomplished an awful lot in thirty years."
I tried to be a boost, but she was lost in a world of groans.

"Thirty years old . . . thirty years old . . . thirty years
old. . . ."

Later that evening I decided on a plan of action. *To
soften the blow of her thirtieth birthday, I'll put together a
giant celebration,* I thought.

I checked my calendar and my bank account. I was
doing a good amount of weekend speaking around the
country in the next few weeks. The extra money would be

175

just the help I needed to pull off a birthday worth remembering.

The following few weeks were so much fun. I secretly shopped by phone. I snuck out to stores to check out different styles and prices. I was making progress, and Rhonda was clueless.

Finally her birthday week arrived. I frantically finished phoning. "Let me be very clear," I'd say over the phone. "This merchandise must arrive at our house on Thursday. Friday is too late." They all agreed to my plan.

Rhonda's birthday was Saturday, but my plan called for a three-day blowout in honor of the thirtieth birthday of the Teacher of the Year.

"Something special is going to happen today in honor of your birthday!" I told Rhonda Thursday morning as I was walking out the door to go to work. "Be prepared!"

I would call periodically throughout the day. No delivery. I came home for lunch. No delivery. Early afternoon, no delivery. I started to panic. I made some more phone calls and prayed like crazy.

About 4:20 that afternoon I got the call I'd been waiting for.

"Bill? You're so sweet. I'm gonna cry! They're beautiful!"

"What's that?" I asked, purposely playing dumb.

"You know," she chided, "the furniture store just delivered two beautiful chairs for our bedroom. They fit just perfectly over in the corner. We finally have a quiet place to sit and talk!"

She was very happy. I was overjoyed.

"I need to run out and get some groceries for dinner," she informed me. "But I'll be right back."

"Babe, no," I insisted. "This is the beginning of your birthday celebration. I'll be home in about twenty minutes and I'll take care of dinner."

She agreed—reluctantly—but she agreed.

I packed my briefcase and hit the highway. As I was driving home I kept praying, *Lord, please see to it that the rest of the surprise arrives . . . soon. Please? Amen.*

I turned the corner and headed up the street to Union Avenue. Rhonda was standing in our front yard. I could tell by her look God had answered my prayer.

Her face was soaked. She was laughing, sobbing, shaking, totally out of control.

"Oh, babe!" She grabbed me out of the car and squeezed me tighter than I could ever recall. "How did you do all this without me knowing? All of it is absolutely beautiful! Come in and take a look!"

She reached for my hand and walked me through the front door to see the rest of her Thursday surprise.

The living room was no longer naked. It was now dressed quite nicely in beautiful new furniture.

That evening we enjoyed the first of a very popular pastime at Union Station. We sat on our new couch, purposely positioned right in front of the fireplace.

Friday was Day 2 of the three-day blowout. "I'll be home by 4:45," I instructed Rhonda. "Please be ready for me. By that I mean please be dressed to kill. We're going out for a night on the town!"

"Dressed to kill," is only an expression. But when I arrived home that evening, I thought I really needed the paramedics.

Rhonda was absolutely stunning.

"We're out to give schoolteachers a new image!" I said as I beamed with pride. "You're beautiful! Incredibly gorgeous!"

With the baby-sitter the only other adult privy to our night's location, Rhonda and I began our evening with dinner at her favorite restaurant. It's really our "special occasion" restaurant. Boy, this was special.

"Everyone is staring at us," I said as I leaned over the table. "They are all mumbling something about how such an ugly cuss could be escorting such a radiant beauty!" Rhonda blushed, reached over, and squeezed my hand. I continued: "Well, I won't let them talk about you like that. You have every right to be with a beauty like me!"

The squeeze from her hand became a kick into my shin. "Just kidding!" I quickly added. And she knew it. People really were staring. For she was truly radiantly beautiful.

From there it was off to an evening at the theatre. Now at Union Station, an evening at the theatre usually means down to the local movie house, where you pay one dollar to see movies that just went off cable. But tonight was different. We drove down into Los Angeles to attend *live* theatre. A musical . . . Rhonda's favorite form of entertainment. It was wonderfully captivating. A splendid production.

Saturday arrived and the kids all cheered. This was *their* day to be involved in the giant, three-day birthday bash for Mama.

We all went to a local café for a birthday breakfast. We do this for every family member's birthday. The special treat is that the birthday person gets to order steak and eggs. The rest of us eat a steakless breakfast in honor of the day.

There was lots of laughter and kissing and hugs. When we got back home, the kids ran off to work on a theatrical production of their own to perform for Mama that evening.

We had a simple dinner that evening, saving room for ice cream and cake. The kids individually presented Mama with their homemade gifts. She was just as touched by these inexpensive items as she was by the costly furniture. I was so pleased to see that happen. Tears were flowing freely.

Finally it was time for the dramatic production. With all the tears flowing, the song the kids had written was quite appropriate.

They came out with umbrellas, a la Gene Kelly, and sang a song in praise of Rhonda. There were lyrics that came and went, but the chorus they sang over and over went like this:

"Singing in the rain with you—WORLD'S GREATEST MOM!
Singing in the rain with you—WORLD'S GREATEST MOM!"

Those four—oops—*five* kids really believe Rhonda is the world's greatest mom. I observed this scene and looked carefully into the eyes of my wife. There were costs, there were frustrations, there were trade-offs—

But it is worth it all,
. . . to be the "World's Greatest Mom."

Union Station Recommendations

More and more material is being made available to home-schooling families. Here are some sources that were very helpful to us.

The biggest help was Susan Schaeffer Macaulay's book *For The Children's Sake*. It is published by Crossway Books in Westchester, Illinois 60153.

The books by Raymond and Dorothy Moore are also very thought provoking. *Home Grown Kids, Home Spun Schools*, and *Home Style Teaching* are all published by Word Books in Waco, Texas. *Better Late Than Early* is available through the Hewitt Research Foundation in Berrien Springs, Michigan 49103.

We're very pleased with the curriculum we obtain from the Calvert School, Tuscany Road, Baltimore, Maryland 21210. They have good stuff for all grades.

Jeffrey learned to read with the help of a program called *Sing, Spell, Read and Write*. Their material is available by writing *Sing, Spell, Read and Write*, c/o CBN, Virginia Beach, Virginia 23463.

You can get more information on The God Hunt by writing David and Karen Mains at The Chapel of the Air, Box 30, Wheaton, Illinois 60189. The book *The God Hunt* was published by David C. Cook Publishing Company, Elgin, Illinois 60120.

If I can be of help to you, write me in care of Fleming H. Revell, Old Tappan, New Jersey 07675.